HERITAGE OF
EVIDENCE

Heritage *of* Evidence

in the British Museum

Peter Masters

THE WAKEMAN TRUST, LONDON

HERITAGE OF EVIDENCE

© Peter Masters 2004

This guide started life as a tour-scheme in the early 1960s, and has since been serialised several times in Christian periodicals, and also issued in magazine format. This fully revised edition takes account of Museum gallery changes to the date of publication. It includes a number of discoveries, with explanations, not in the British Museum.

Most photographs by Chris Laws
Design and preparation by Hannah Wyncoll and Esther Harris
Cover design by Andrew Owen

THE WAKEMAN TRUST
(UK Registered Charity)

Website: www.wakemantrust.org

UK Registered Office
38 Walcot Square
London SE11 4TZ

US Office
300 Artino Drive
Oberlin, OH 44074-1263

ISBN 1 870855 39 6

Printed by Stephens & George, Merthyr Tydfil, UK

SCHEME OF CONTENTS

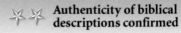

Other books by Dr Peter Masters
are listed on the publisher's website:
www.wakemantrust.org

Sermons of Dr Masters, audio or video,
may be downloaded or viewed on the website of
the Metropolitan Tabernacle:
www.metropolitantabernacle.org

THE BRITISH MUSEUM
is in Great Russell Street
London WC1
Tel: 020 7323 8000

The Museum website is:
www.thebritishmuseum.ac.uk

Details of opening times and facilities
are publicised on this website

(This book is not a British Museum publication)

THE BRITISH MUSEUM holds a huge number of major discoveries that provide direct corroboration and background confirmation for an immense sweep of Bible history. This survey of Bible-authenticating exhibits has been designed as a guide for visitors, and also to give pleasure and interest to readers unable to tour the galleries. In a couple of hours or more it is possible to tour a selection of exhibits which constitute an outstanding summary of the whole field of archaeological discovery relating to the Bible. In today's atheistic climate most people have no idea how much powerful evidence exists for the literal accuracy of the biblical record.

It is true that the best evidence for the divine inspiration and infallibility of the Bible is to be found within the Bible itself, such as its unique explanation of the human condition, its fulfilled prophecies, its remarkable self-consistent character, its profound teaching, as well as other exclusive attributes marking it out as God's book.

Yet there are many benefits to be derived from reviewing archaeological discoveries that confirm the historical accuracy of the Bible, because these discoveries reassure seekers, illuminate events and decisively refute the claims of cynics. May this guide be helpful for group visits and personal reading, stimulating for many a new appreciation of the uniqueness of the Scriptures.

Excavations at Nineveh

Sir Austen Henry Layard, British diplomat, catapulted to fame as an archaeologist by his momentous excavations of Assyrian palaces 150 years ago, was no mean artist. This is his watercolour entitled 'Excavations at Nineveh'.

The Route is Important

The route followed in this book has been used (and updated) for very large groups of adults, students, seminarians, and other young people, for more than forty years.

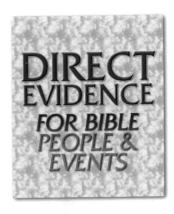

Some biblical evidence tours take a different route in an effort to follow the order of Bible history, beginning in the upstairs galleries with Abraham's boyhood city of Ur, and going on to Egyptian exhibits, and so on. The problem with this route is that the visitor sees much less *direct* authentication of Bible events for the first half of the tour. Only in the second half, when pretty tired, does the visitor make it to the most stunning exhibits of all. (Furthermore, the chronological aim is soon frustrated by the layout of the galleries and cannot be maintained.)

We therefore begin in Assyria with some of the most powerful direct 'proofs' of biblical people and events. This is the best order for people taking an enquiring interest in the authenticity of the

Bible, as well as for students, for whom any museum still evokes 'school-trip' syndrome. Subsequently, visitors are able to appreciate all other exhibits in a more focused way.

Because we begin with the ninth century BC – the interaction between Assyria and Israel – time charts are provided throughout the book to maintain perspective.

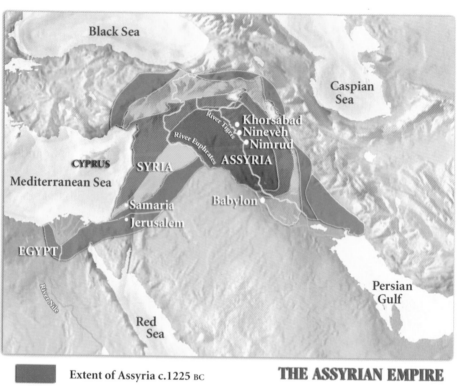

Extent of Assyria c.1225 BC

THE ASSYRIAN EMPIRE

Expansion 858-824 BC (Shalmaneser III)

745-727 BC (Tiglath-pileser III)

721-681 BC (Sargon II and Sennacherib)

Assyrian Empire at the height of its power 680-626 BC

THROUGHOUT THIS BOOK NUMBERS IN SQUARE BRACKETS
FOLLOWING THE NAMES OF ARTEFACTS ARE THE BRITISH MUSEUM'S IDENTIFYING
NUMBERS. WE PROVIDE THESE TO AVOID CONFUSION BETWEEN ITEMS,
AND TO ASSIST IN THEIR LOCATION IN THE EVENT OF
EXHIBITS BEING MOVED.

How Assyrian Monuments Confirm the Bible

The first leg of this tour surveys discoveries found mostly in the excavations of Assyrian royal palaces. From around 880 BC the Assyrian empire really began to take shape bringing terror and tyranny for nearly three centuries, and engulfing many other kingdoms. Several Assyrian kings invaded or threatened the Bible lands of Israel and Judah, securing submission and tribute from them. Many years of such interaction naturally led to various names and battles being mentioned in both the Bible and the annals and monuments of the Assyrians, confirming the historical accuracy of the biblical record.

We begin this tour turning immediately left inside the Museum entrance and proceeding past the cloakroom to Room 6, the Assyrian Sculpture Gallery, to see the first of many highly significant discoveries.

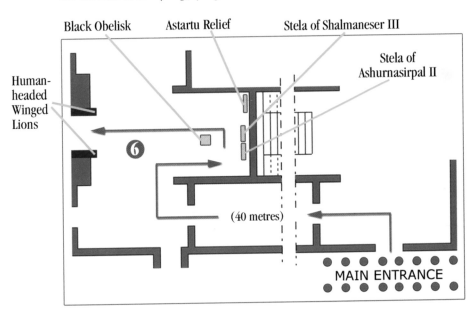

Shalmaneser Names Ahab and Benhadad 853 BC

THESE PAGES

DATES
853 BC

CHIEF PEOPLE
Ashurnasirpal II
Shalmaneser III
Ahab, king of Israel
Benhadad, king of Syria

AT THE TIME OF
Elisha

BOOKS OF BIBLE
1 Kings 22

Turn immediately right as you enter Room 6 and walk to the end wall.

One of the first items we view is an Assyrian monument mentioning the names of two kings who feature prominently in the Old Testament, and confirming the integrity of biblical dating. Three similar monuments stand together, one of which (in the middle) commemorates Ashurnasirpal II (883-859 BC), the Assyrian king who began the policy of expansion and empire building. He introduced new siege techniques to Assyrian warfare, particularly the use of earth ramparts and battering engines, supported by sling-shooters and archers.

To the left of him is a sandy-coloured monument of tremendous importance to us. It is known as the *Stela of Shalmaneser III* (also called the *Kurkh Stele*). This shows Shalmaneser III (who ruled Assyria from 859-824 BC) saluting his gods symbolised in the small pictures above his hand. Writing appears all over the king's picture and also on the back of the monument. This text describes Shalmaneser's first six military campaigns, including specific mention of Ahab (king of Israel) and Benhadad I (king of Syria).

He records how (in 853 BC) he ventured west threatening many kingdoms, but the king of Hamath organised a mighty defence force supplied by twelve kings (Ahab and Benhadad being among them). These two spent most of their time at war with each other, but during a three-year peace (mentioned in *1 Kings 22.1*) they joined forces with Hamath to repel Shalmaneser. (This was during the ministry of the prophet Elisha.) An engagement was fought at Karkara (also spelt Qarqara) near Hamath. In this monument, Shalmaneser describes it in these words:

Left: The Stela of Shalmaneser III [ANE 118884] in Room 6

Below: The Stela of Ashurnasirpal II [ANE 118883] in Room 6

'I approached Karkara. I destroyed, tore down, and bound Karkara, his royal residence. He brought along to help him 1,200 chariots, 1,200 cavalrymen, 20,000 foot soldiers belonging to Hadadezer [Benhadad I] of Damascus, . . . 2,000 chariots, 10,000 foot soldiers belonging to Ahab the Israelite . . .'

The text records that the whole confederate army had 50,000 infantry, 14,000 cavalry and nearly 4,000 chariots. Shalmaneser boasts that he won such a great victory that the rivers were dammed with corpses and the valleys flowed with blood, but his victory could not have been quite as dramatic as this because his advance was effectively halted and he never took possession of his enemy's territory. Nor does the Bible mention that either Ahab or Benhadad suffered a military set-back on such a scale. Shortly after this event Ahab returned to the offensive against Benhadad and died on the battlefield *(1 Kings 22.34-35)*.

Such inscriptions as these provide a definite confirmation that the various people described in *2 Kings* and *2 Chronicles* were true historical figures. As we shall see, this monument is typical of so much which has been unearthed confirming that biblical characters lived at the times and in the places stated in the Bible.

Tiglath-pileser Invades Israel 734 –732 BC

To the left of the Stela of Shalmaneser III is a slab relief from Nimrud showing the capture of Astartu in 732 BC.

After the death of the Assyrian emperor Shalmaneser III in 824 BC, nearly eighty years passed without serious trouble between Assyria and Palestine. Then in 745 BC an Assyrian general seized power, assuming the lordly name of Tiglath-pileser III, and resuming the aggressive policies of Shalmaneser III. Tiglath invaded Israel twice during his reign. The limestone relief before us tells of the capture of Astartu (a place in Gilead, east of the river Jordan). Specifically, it commemorates Tiglath's second invasion of Israel

THESE PAGES

DATES
732 BC

CHIEF PEOPLE
Tiglath-pileser III
Pekah, king of Israel

AT THE TIME OF
Isaiah
Hosea

BOOKS OF BIBLE
2 Kings 15.29
1 Chronicles 5.25-26

Relief from the palace at Nimrud recording the capture of Astartu in Gilead
[ANE 118908], in Room 6.

between 734-732 BC. The king is shown at the bottom, while above him booty and Israelite prisoners are being led away. This totally corroborates the biblical record of *2 Kings 15.29*, which reads:

> 'In the days of Pekah king of Israel came Tiglath-pileser king of Assyria, and took Ijon, and Abel-beth-maachah, and Janoah, and Kedesh, and Hazor, and Gilead, and Galilee, all the land of Naphtali, and carried them captive to Assyria.'

1 Chronicles 5.25-26 also refers to this punitive invasion of Israel by Tiglath-pileser (in this passage he is called 'Pul'). This invasion is also confirmed by the tablet recording Tiglath's annals to be seen shortly in a lower room [WA K 3751], see page 46.

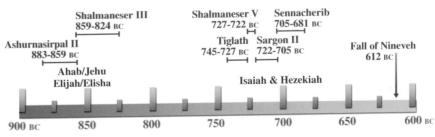

Shalmaneser Provides Jehu's Portrait 841 BC

The Black Obelisk

(Standing behind us as we viewed the previous items)

This takes us back to the time of Shalmaneser III, and provides the only known picture of a Hebrew king. It is a black, limestone pillar (about 6½ feet tall) with four sides covered with pictures and writing, recording (among other things) how Jehu king of Israel paid homage to Shalmaneser. Jehu is named and shown prostrating himself before him, and the text states the value of the homage:

ASSYRIAN QUOTE

'I received from him silver, gold, a golden bowl, golden goblets, pitchers of gold, tin, a staff for the hand of the king . . .'

Background

After the death of Ahab (king of Israel) in 853 BC, his son, Ahaziah, ruled for two years, dying prematurely in 852 BC, then another son Jehoram (or Joram) ruled for ten years. This was an intensely evil reign, and in 841 BC a military captain named Jehu was 'anointed' king of Israel by Elisha's messenger, and commanded to destroy the Ahab dynasty. All this is recorded in *2 Kings 9* and *10*. Jehu went on to reign for 28 years, beginning a dynasty of some 100 years.

Jehu took a chariot to the town of Jezreel where Ahab's son, King Joram (recovering from battle wounds) was accompanied by another Ahaziah, the twenty-one year old king of Judah (a hopeless and wicked individual). Jehu's chariot raised such a cloud of dust that the Jezreel town watchman thought it was a large company approaching. However, as Jehu drew nearer, he reported – 'The driving is like the driving of Jehu . . . for he driveth furiously'

THESE PAGES

DATES
853–841 BC

CHIEF PEOPLE
Shalmaneser III
Joram, king of Israel
Jehu, king of Israel

AT THE TIME OF
Elisha

BOOKS OF BIBLE
2 Kings 8–10

The Black Obelisk of Shalmaneser III
(Jehu is in second frame from the top)
[ANE 118885] in Room 6.

(2 Kings 9.20). Jehu shot
Joram with an arrow as he
tried to escape, and also
fatally wounded Ahaziah.
He entered the town and
found the notorious Jezebel,
Ahab's widow, who had
'painted her face' and was
looking out of an upper
window. He ordered her to
be unceremoniously
thrown out of the window
to her death, and dogs ate
her flesh.

Jehu set about purging
Baal worship out of Israel
with considerable cunning
and violence, exterminat-
ing all the failed royal
house of Israel, and the

The Black Obelisk close up showing Jehu bringing tribute
to Shalmaneser [ANE 118885], in Room 6.

priests of Baal. From this obelisk, we learn that Jehu (in the first year
of his reign) attempted to buy the friendship of Assyria by paying
homage to Shalmaneser III.

In this monument, discovered in 1845 at Nimrud, the existence of
yet another Bible king receives solid corroboration from a contem-
porary secular record.

We now turn to face the pair of *human-headed winged lions* which once
flanked the doorway of the throne room of Ashurnasirpal II, king of Assyria
883-859 BC (before Shalmaneser III). His palace was at Nimrud. The next
pages sketch the history of the three Assyrian capitals with their palaces.

Room 6 – Assyrian Sculpture

Artist's impression of the Royal Palace at Nimrud

Assyrian Royal Palaces 880-612 BC

Assyrian kings flanked the entrances to their royal palaces with colossal, human-headed winged bulls and lions. These were designed to project an image of intelligence and power, and to signify the emperor's extensive dominions. These huge human-headed lions from Nimrud (which we see here) 'guarded' the palaces of several kings who invaded and oppressed Bible lands. The walled city of Nimrud covered 890 acres. The palace alone covered 50 acres, building activities lasting 50 years.

The huge *Gates of Balawat* (a secondary palace built for Shalmaneser III) were decorated with bands of engraved bronze, the originals of which are in glass cases on either side of a modern reproduction of the gates. One of these bronze bands also features the military expedition against Karkara (see page 12). Chariots are shown attacking the region of Hamath, and below, captives are being led away. **Look for a case on the left as you go between the winged lions [Band 124655].**

The history of the three significant Assyrian capitals, Nimrud,

Band 124655

ANE 118872

Above: Bronze band from the Gates of Balawat, the palace of Shalmaneser III, recording and validating hostilities at Hamath (upper portion) and Karkara (lower) described on page 12; in Room 6. **Right:** Human-headed winged bull, one of a pair, guarding Ashurnasirpal II's palace; in Room 8.

ANE 118801-2

Reconstruction of the Gates of Balawat with a pair of human-headed winged (5-legged) lions from the doorway of Ashurnasirpal II's throne room at Nimrud; in Room 6.

Khorsabad and Nineveh, is easy to sketch. The Assyrian capital was moved from Ashur to Nimrud by Ashurnasirpal II about 880 BC, and this continued to be the capital for 170 years. When Shalmaneser III ascended the throne he added the secondary palace at nearby Balawat. After five relatively insignificant kings, Tiglath-pileser III ascended the Assyrian throne in 745 BC. He invaded Israel and recorded his exploits as we have seen. Tiglath-pileser reigned from Nimrud, and would have regularly passed by these winged creatures. His son Shalmaneser V also reigned from Nimrud.

It was not until Shalmaneser V was succeeded by Sargon II in 722 BC, that Nimrud ceased to be the capital of Assyria, Sargon building a new palace for himself at Khorsabad. (His winged bulls turn up shortly in this tour.) Khorsabad, however, lasted for only one reign, because Sargon's son, Sennacherib, moved the capital to Nineveh. This remained the capital through the reigns of five more kings until its destruction by the Chaldeans in 612 BC.

The order, then, for Assyrian palaces connected with Bible history is – Nimrud 880-710 BC (including nearby Balawat from about 845 BC); Khorsabad 710-700 BC; and Nineveh 700-612 BC.

Nimrud Wall Sculptures

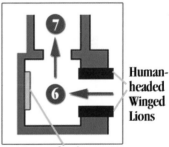

From the Gates of Balawat, we turn into Room 7, Nimrud Palace Reliefs (which used to be called the Nimrud Gallery).

Here are bas-reliefs from the throne room of the palace of Ashurnasirpal II. The extreme barbarity of this king towards his rebels and defeated enemies exceeds anything in history. The main features of these panels are the king hunting and campaigning. There being no direct evidence for biblical events here, we pass swiftly through to Room 8.

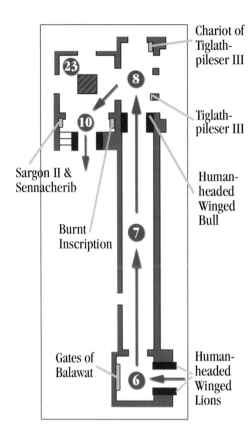

Chariot of Tiglath-pileser III

Tiglath-pileser III

Human-headed Winged Bull

Sargon II & Sennacherib

Burnt Inscription

Gates of Balawat

Human-headed Winged Lions

THESE PAGES

DATES
745–727 BC

CHIEF PEOPLE
Tiglath-pileser III
Menahem, Pekah &
Hoshea, kings of Israel
Ahaz, king of Judah
Rezin, king of Syria

AT THE TIME OF
Isaiah
Hosea

BOOKS OF BIBLE
2 Kings 15-16
2 Chronicles 28
Isaiah 7

Room 8 (more Nimrud Palace Reliefs) has other giant human-headed beasts, but we are interested in Tiglath-pileser III.

More on Tiglath-pileser III ('Pul') 745-727 BC

We met Tiglath when viewing the *Astartu Relief* which commemorated his second invasion of Israel in 732 BC. He is mentioned nine times in the Bible, and his portrait in stone is here on the right as we emerge from Room 7. Further ahead on the right is a bas-relief depicting the *Chariot of Tiglath-pileser III*.

The first of Tiglath's invasions is recorded in *2 Kings 15.19-20*. At the time Israel's king was Menahem (who reigned 752-742 BC). The Bible says:

> 'Pul the king of Assyria came against the land: and Menahem gave Pul a thousand talents of silver, that his hand might be with him ...and Menahem exacted the money of Israel, even of all the mighty men of wealth, of each man fifty shekels of silver ... so the king of Assyria turned back.'

Tiglath-pileser's own annals (not on view here) say:

ASSYRIAN QUOTE

'As for Menahem, I overwhelmed him like a snowstorm and he fled like a bird alone, and bowed to my feet. I returned him to his place and imposed tribute upon him.'

Other annals of this Assyrian king further corroborate the Bible's account of his invasion of Israel. We provide, for interest, this résumé of events drawn from *2 Kings 15.22-31; 16.5-9; 2 Chronicles 28* and *Isaiah 7*, followed by some references to Tiglath-pileser's own remarkable records:

Pekah, a military commander, began to reign in Israel in 740 BC

Left: Tiglath-pileser III [WA 118900] in Room 8

Below: Another version of Tiglath-pileser III's chariot [WA 124961 & 132306] in Room 8

following a murderous coup. Within a few years he joined forces with Rezin, the king of Syria, and began to attack Judah. Down in Judah, King Ahaz ignored Isaiah's advice and refused to look to God for help. Consequently, the Israel-Syria alliance wounded Judah severely, slaying 120,000 men and taking many captives. In desperation Ahaz turned to Tiglath-pileser of Assyria and paid him to come to his rescue. His message read:

> 'I am thy servant and thy son: come up, and save me out of the hand of the king of Syria, and out of the hand of the king of Israel, which rise up against me. And Ahaz took the silver and gold . . . found in the house of the Lord, and in the treasures of the king's house, and sent it . . . to the king of Assyria. And . . . the king of Assyria went up against Damascus, and took it . . . and slew Rezin' *(2 Kings 16.7-9)*.

So, in 732 BC, the alliance of Pekah (of Israel) and Rezin (of Damascus, Syria) was broken. Damascus fell, and the long history of the kingdom of Syria was brought to an end. As for Pekah, at precisely the same time he fell victim to a conspiracy at home when Hoshea put him to death and took the throne *(2 Kings 15.30)*.

Tiglath-pileser's annals confirm all this, referring to the following people and events. In an inscription he tells how Ahaz (of Judah) paid him an enormous tax of royal treasure, gold, silver, lead, tin, iron, woollen goods, linen, purple, trained horses and mules. Tiglath also gives details of how he took Syria, conquering all the way to Damascus. He tells of how King Rezin fled into the city, and how, amidst scenes of devastation and destruction, Rezin's advisers were

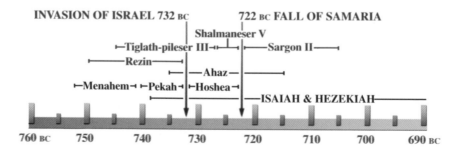

impaled. Tiglath-pileser's annals also refer to the assassination of Pekah, claiming a part in the conspiracy in these words: 'They overthrew their king Pekah and I placed Hoshea over them as king.' The historical nature of the biblical narrative could not be more comprehensively confirmed.

Sargon II and the Fall of Samaria 722 BC

From Room 8 we enter Room 23 (Greek and Roman Sculpture), turning left into Room 10, where colossal human-headed bulls from the city gates at Khorsabad stand guard. On our level at the top of a flight of stairs is a larger-than-life representation of Assyrian emperor Sargon II, whose records confirm the biblical account of the fall of Samaria, the capital of the northern kingdom of Israel, in 722 BC. This great sculpture from Sargon's palace at Khorsabad shows the king on the left receiving a nobleman, most probably crown prince Sennacherib, his son.

In *2 Kings 17.1-6* we read of how Hoshea, the king of Israel, initially submitted to the yoke of Shalmaneser V and paid tribute to him. Before long, however, Hoshea stopped paying the tribute and appealed to Egypt to help him resist Assyria. Shalmaneser reacted by seizing Hoshea, imprisoning him and laying siege to the city of Samaria. This fell after three years in 722 BC – immediately after Shalmaneser had died and been succeeded by Sargon II.

Sargon II is therefore the Assyrian emperor who claims to have directed the final fall, punishment and captivity of the kingdom of Israel, following centuries of warning from the prophets. Thus the

THESE PAGES
DATES
722 BC
CHIEF PEOPLE
Shalmaneser V
Sargon II
Hoshea, king of Israel
AT THE TIME OF
Isaiah
Hosea
BOOKS OF BIBLE
2 Kings 17.1-6, 24
Isaiah 20.1

Wall panel showing Sargon II (left) receiving a high official, probably Sennacherib [ANE 118822], in Room 10.

ten northern tribes went into captivity, leaving only the southern kingdom of Judah in freedom. Samaria had withstood the siege for three years due to its unusually strong fortifications. Excavations show that forty to fifty years before the siege of 722 BC, King Jeroboam had given the city a double wall with an overall thickness of up to 32 feet. Nevertheless, as the Bible says, Samaria fell because of the wickedness of the people, and –

BIBLE
QUOTE

'The king of Assyria took Samaria, and carried Israel away into Assyria . . . and the king of Assyria brought men from Babylon, and from Cuthah, and from Ava, and from Hamath, and from Sepharvaim, and placed them in the cities of Samaria instead of the children of Israel' *(2 Kings 17.6 and 24).*

Sargon II took the credit for the fall of Samaria, in several inscriptions, such as an inscribed prism [WA 22505] held in the Museum but not on display. This traces an expedition of Sargon II against various places including Palestine, claiming the conquest of

Samaria, 'the land of the house of Omri'. Another inscription left by Sargon II says:

ASSYRIAN QUOTE

> 'In the first year of my reign I besieged and conquered Samaria, and carried away 27,290 inhabitants.'

These words are from the *Sargon Inscription*, discovered at Khorsabad, now in the Louvre, Paris. A very comprehensive description is on a prism in the Iraq Museum, Baghdad (and fortunately not looted). It includes this passage about Samaria:

ASSYRIAN QUOTE

> 'I surrounded and deported as prisoners 27,290 of its inhabitants . . . From them I equipped 200 chariots for my own army units . . . I restored the city of Samaria . . . I brought into it people from the countries conquered by my own hands.'

The precision of the biblical narrative is thus totally vindicated by several ancient documents. The people brought into Samaria to replace Israelites were Assyrian prisoners taken from Babylon and Northern Syria. These gave rise to new languages and customs, with much religious confusion. The result was the cult of the Samaritans, from whom the mainstream Jews of Judah stood aloof.

Inscribed prism of Sargon II in the Iraq Museum, Baghdad, describing the fall and repopulating of Samaria, confirming *2 Kings 17*. (The British Museum's undisplayed prism [WA 22505] is similar, but nonagonal.)

Room 10 – Khorsabad Palace Reliefs and Assyrian Sculpture

The King of Moab Confirms Bible History c. 853 BC

The Moabite Stone (Mesha's Stele)

THESE PAGES

DATES
  c. 853 BC

CHIEF PEOPLE
  Mesha, king of Moab
  Omri & Ahab, kings of
  Israel

AT THE TIME OF
  Elisha

BOOKS OF BIBLE
  2 Kings 3.4-5

The *Moabite Stone* cannot be seen in the British Museum, although for years an actual-size copy was exhibited. We mention it here because it is one of the most sensational memorials to turn up, throwing light on Bible history. The original stone is exhibited in the Louvre, Paris. The land of Moab lay east of the Dead Sea, and was roughly 600 miles long by 25-30 miles wide. David and Solomon subdued it as a vassal state, but after 930 BC it threw off the yoke of Israel. However, the Bible records that by 853 BC (the year Ahab died) Moab had long been subdued once again by Israel, and was preparing for a second attempt at independence. *2 Kings 3.4-5* tells us:

> 'And Mesha king of Moab was a sheepmaster, and rendered unto the king of Israel 100,000 lambs, and 100,000 rams, with the wool. But it came to pass, when Ahab was dead, that the king of Moab rebelled against the king of Israel.'

In 1868 this ancient memorial stone came into the possession of an Arab sheikh, confirming the accuracy of the text quoted, naming the Israelite kings Omri and Ahab, and providing a list of the accomplishments of Mesha, the Moabite king. In 39 lines of writing he tells us:

> 'I am Mesha . . . king of Moab . . . As for Omri, king of Israel, he humbled Moab many years . . . and his son [Ahab] . . . also said, I will humble Moab. In my time he thus spoke, but I have triumphed over him . . .'

The *Moabite Stone* goes on to speak of the taking of other districts

[362]

The Moabite Stone, also known as Mesha's Stele, is nearly 4 feet high, 2 feet wide, and 2½ inches thick.

from Israel, and of the building of reservoirs and townships. It is certainly a most significant confirmation of the accuracy of the historical details in the Bible.

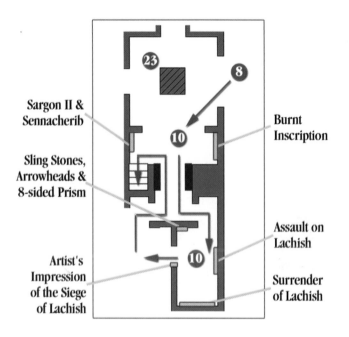

Sargon II &
Sennacherib

Sling Stones,
Arrowheads &
8-sided Prism

Artist's
Impression
of the Siege
of Lachish

Burnt
Inscription

Assault on
Lachish

Surrender
of Lachish

Hezekiah's Defence of Jerusalem 701 BC

…as described in the chronicles and palace sculptures of King Sennacherib

THESE PAGES

DATES
701 BC

CHIEF PEOPLE
Sennacherib
Hezekiah, king of Judah
Isaiah

BOOKS OF BIBLE
2 Kings 18-20
2 Chronicles 32
Isaiah 36-37

Opposite the relief of Sargon II and Sennacherib is a large, scorched inscribed panel (to be described on opposite page).

The Lachish room shortly to be entered displays one of the most spectacular confirmations of Bible history ever unearthed. Indeed, these items from the palace of Nineveh were the very first *direct* proof found of an event in Bible history when discovered in 1847. Sennacherib, king of Assyria, was even more aggressive than his father Sargon II. In 701 BC he swept into Judah with a massive army and proceeded to capture all her fortress cities. At the time Isaiah was resident prophet in Jerusalem, and Hezekiah was king. Sennacherib's encounter with the outstanding and godly Hezekiah receives considerable coverage in the Bible. It is also one of the best

Reconstruction of the siege of Lachish by Alan Sorrell, in Room 10.

documented events in the Assyrian records. Sennacherib's chronicles were found at Nineveh together with the pictures in stone which lined the walls of his 71-roomed palace.

We look first at the very large slab, covered in text, just outside the Lachish room (pictured overleaf). It is badly scorched because nearly 100 years later, in 612 BC, Nineveh was destroyed by fire (just as Nahum had prophesied). The text gives details of the tribute sent by Hezekiah to the Assyrians, and accounted for after the campaign. The Bible tells us that Hezekiah had refused to serve and pay the king of Assyria *(2 Kings 18.1-8)*. Sennacherib's anger was aroused, as *2 Kings 18.13-15* relates (here paraphrased) –

BIBLE PARAPHRASE

> Now in the fourteenth year of king Hezekiah, Sennacherib king of Assyria came up against all the walled cities of Judah, and took them. And Hezekiah sent to the king of Assyria, at Lachish, saying, I have offended; return from me: whatever penalty you impose on me I will bear. And the king of Assyria imposed on Hezekiah 300 talents of silver and 30 talents of gold. Also Hezekiah gave him all the silver that was in the house of the Lord and the treasures of the king's house.

Burnt Inscription from Nineveh south-west palace recording Hezekiah's tribute to Assyria [WA 118815], in Room 10

The tribute imposed upon Hezekiah amounted to 22,500 pounds weight of silver and 2,250 pounds of gold. Despite having extracted this enormous payment, Sennacherib evidently decided to continue with his attempt to sack Jerusalem, and sent his senior commander to say so, while he continued to besiege Lachish, the last fortified city on the main road to Jerusalem from the south-west, and 30 miles away (this is all in *2 Kings 18.17-37*).

Sennacherib's annals mainly agree with the Bible's account of the conflict (we shall see these in the *Taylor Prism* later). In them, the Assyrian says –

ASSYRIAN QUOTE

'As for Hezekiah the Jew, who did not submit to my yoke, 46 of his strong, walled cities ... by escalade and by bringing up siege engines, by attacking and storming ... by mines, tunnels and breaches, I besieged and took. 200,150 people ... horses ... cattle and sheep without number I brought away ...

'*[Hezekiah]* himself like a caged bird I shut up in Jerusalem, his royal city. Earthworks I threw up against him; the one coming out of his city gate I turned back to his misery ...

'As for Hezekiah, the terrifying splendour of my majesty overcame him ... and his mercenary troops ... deserted him. In addition to 30 talents of gold and 800 talents of silver *[I took]* gems, antimony, jewels ... ivory ... valuable treasures, as well as his daughters, his harem, his male and female musicians which I sent to Nineveh, my royal city.'

Archaeologist's drawing of Fortress-Lachish before it fell to Sennacherib.

The 19th-century archaeologist Sir Henry Layard, who discovered Nineveh, made numerous remarkable drawings of the sculptures underground, before their removal. This is his drawing of the siege of Lachish which may be compared with the actual sculptures in the Lachish room (see picture opposite and descriptions of events in the text).

The Bible and Sennacherib's inscriptions agree that (1) Hezekiah rebelled, (2) that precisely 46 walled cities of Judah fell, (3) Lachish also fell, (4) Hezekiah was 'shut up' in Jerusalem *by events*, (5) 30 talents of gold were paid in tribute (though the precise amount of silver and other items are in dispute), and (6) Jerusalem itself did not fall, the mighty Assyrian army leaving the area without an engagement there. In the Bible's account, Sennacherib's army was destroyed by the angel of the Lord, while the Assyrian version (on the famous *Taylor Prism*) gives implicit acknowledgement that Jerusalem remained intact. Points of disagreement are easily accounted for.

We now pass between Sargon's winged bulls and enter the room containing the *Lachish Reliefs*. Jerusalem never fell, and so Sennacherib had to be content with Lachish as the subject of his sculptures. Furthermore, he never returned to the region of Palestine, doubtless due to the severity of his losses. The Bible relates how Hezekiah made thorough preparations for a seemingly inevitable siege of

Jerusalem. He prayed for God's help, and Isaiah gave him a word from the Lord assuring him of deliverance. All this is recorded in detail in *2 Kings 18-19*, *2 Chronicles 32*, and *Isaiah 36-37*. There was an interlude when Sennacherib was called away to deal with an offensive by Tirhakah, then crown prince or king-regent of Ethiopia (referred to in *2 Kings 19.9* and *Isaiah 37.9*). It must have been on its return that the Assyrian army was destroyed before it ever reached the walls of Jerusalem. One night –

> 'the angel of the Lord went out, and smote in the camp of the Assyrians 185,000 . . . So Sennacherib king of Assyria departed' *(2 Kings 19.35-36).*

The Lachish room gives a very vivid idea of the barbaric and terrifying siege warfare employed by Sennacherib. The sculptured slabs arranged round this gallery once constituted the 'wallpaper' of one of the palace rooms. They depict the story of the siege and conquest

A scene from the siege of Lachish [WA 124906], in Room 10.

of Lachish from left to right round the room. Sling-shooters are seen behind the assault force, while in front of them are the archers, and then the storm-troopers. Siege engines are being rushed up the massive artificial earth ramparts (which were thrown up under shield cover to effectively reduce the height of the walls). Defenders throw down flaming torches and rocks.

The sculptures show the battle raging on the left of the city, and the result on the right. A chariot and other items are shown being carried out of the city along with numerous prisoners, including carts with families and small children. Dead defenders are shown spiked on poles and paraded about to demoralise others. Some prisoners are being tortured, flayed until the muscles are visible. On the end wall of the gallery Sennacherib is seen on a portable throne receiving the surrender of the city. An inscription reads –

ASSYRIAN QUOTE 'Sennacherib, supreme king, king of Assyria, sits upon a throne while the booty of Lachish passes before him.'

Sennacherib receives the surrender and spoil of Lachish [WA 124910-2], in Room 10.

Left: An eight-sided prism [WA 103000] is displayed in a wall case in Room 10. It includes a report of the capture of Lachish and the effective 'shutting up' of Hezekiah in Jerusalem. The Taylor Prism, which gives Sennacherib's version of his invasion of Judah, is to be seen in the Later Mesopotamia Room (55).

Right: Arrowheads [WA 132146] and sling stones [WA 132127-40] found at the excavation of Lachish, in Room 10.

Perhaps the tribute of Hezekiah was proffered at the same time. The men behind Sennacherib hold fly-whisks; the king's face has been damaged by subsequent vandalism.

In a wall case there is a collection of sling stones and arrowheads found at the excavation of Lachish itself. It is useful to examine the modern artist's impression of the siege which is positioned near the wall case. An eight-sided Assyrian prism (pictured above) records five of Sennacherib's campaigns including the capture of Lachish.

Assassination of Sennacherib

Another fact confirmed in Assyrian records is the biblical account of how Sennacherib returned to Nineveh only to be slain by two of his sons as he worshipped in his idol temple. The Bible also records how these sons fled to Armenia leaving another son, Esarhaddon, to pursue and defeat them, and subsequently to be crowned king. (See *2 Kings 19.36-37; 2 Chronicles 32.21* and *Isaiah 37.38.*)

Assyrian records totally substantiate all this, for in addition to corroboration in the *Babylonian Chronicle,* Esarhaddon's Nineveh records have this inscription:

ASSYRIAN QUOTE

'In the month of Nisanu . . . I made my happy entrance into the royal palace, the awesome place wherein abides the fate of kings. A grim determination fell upon my brothers. They forsook the gods and turned themselves to deeds of violence, scheming evil . . . To seize power they slew Sennacherib their father . . .'

Isaiah the Prophet

With so much archaeological confirmation of the biblical record, we must not lose sight of Isaiah, the towering teacher of the time. He foretold in great detail, 700 years beforehand, how the Messiah would come and suffer to atone for human sin. He spoke of Christ's resurrection, the founding of His church and its worldwide spread. His numerous, very precise predictions, given in soaring prose, have been proved correct, verifying the unique and inspired nature of the Bible. The prophet's chief concern was that individuals should find forgiveness and be reconciled with God.

Hezekiah's Tunnel, Jerusalem

In connection with Hezekiah and Sennacherib, another feature of the Bible narrative has been emphatically confirmed by archaeological discovery. The Bible describes how in 701 BC Hezekiah, in his preparation for siege (possibly after Sennacherib's first offensive), blocked up water sources outside the city and diverted the Gihon Spring via a tunnel to run into the city (*2 Kings 20.20* and *2 Chronicles 32.3-4* and *30).* This 1,748-foot-long tunnel was pickaxed out of

The Siloam Tunnel Inscription in the Archaeological Museum, Istanbul.
Translation shown in panel below.

TUNNEL INSCRIPTION

'This is the way the tunnel was cut through . . . while there remained six cubits to cut through, the voice of one workman *[was heard]* calling to his fellow . . . *[words here seem to indicate that the two tunnels had passed each other slightly]* . . . and when the tunnel was driven through, the workmen struck each toward his fellow, axe against axe, and the water flowed from the spring to the reservoir for 1,200 cubits, and the height of the rock above the head of the workmen was 100 cubits.'

solid limestone rock. About six feet high for most of its length, it lies deep below the surface and leads to the Pool of Siloam (made at the same time). The tunnel was hewn out by two teams working from opposite ends. On completion a commemorative plaque was set into the wall at the point where the workmen met. The tunnel was discovered by Edward Robinson an American orientalist in 1838 and cleared in 1909-11. The inscription which was found in 1880 describes the completion of the tunnel and is pictured above. It is exhibited in the Archaeological Museum, Istanbul.

Hezekiah's Tunnel (also called the Siloam Tunnel) is the prince of the three ancient water systems serving Jerusalem, being by far the longest and deepest of them. An astonishing engineering achievement, completed at breakneck speed, it still defies explanation as to how the workmen, digging from opposite ends, met in the middle, and how they obtained ventilation. It is the longest ancient water tunnel lacking intermediate shafts.

Some geologists had claimed that the tunnel was built in the 2nd century AD, but in 2003 the scientific journal *Nature* published the work of leading geologists affirming an 8th century BC date. This was established by radiocarbon dating of fragments of vegetation in the lime plaster lining, necessary to prevent water loss through fissures in the hewn limestone rock. This lining was up to 8 inches thick.

The tunnel is almost level, descending only 12½ inches in the course of its 1,748 foot length, delivering water to the Siloam Pool. The depth of the tunnel reaches 150 feet. It follows a serpentine track – a feature giving rise to several plausible explanations ranging from the need to avoid underpassing the holy ground of the royal tombs above, to geological constraints.

Left: The Siloam Pool. Boys still swim in the Siloam Pool after 2,700 years. This water has come 1,748 feet from the Gihon Spring outside the city.

Below: Despite sharp curves near the meeting point, as seen here, the two teams of tunnellers working from opposite ends managed to connect near the middle of Hezekiah's Tunnel.

Opposite page: Hezekiah's Tunnel. The ceiling of the tunnel varies in height between 5½ and 6½ feet, although in some places it is as high as 16 feet, the higher area even lacking tool marks, as though the workmen took advantage of a length of natural erosion channel.

Siloam Tunnel pictures by Garo Nalbandian (copyright)

Assyrian King Names Manasseh c. 678 BC

Hezekiah's son, Manasseh, was in turn oppressed by Sennacherib's son Esarhaddon, who invaded Judah (with other territories) imposing painfully heavy tributes of building materials, together with gold and silver, for the rebuilding of his palace at Nineveh. There was no divine deliverance for Manasseh, as there had been for his father, because he had brought back gross idolatry. The Bible says:

BIBLE QUOTE

'So Manasseh made Judah and the inhabitants of Jerusalem to err, and to do worse than the heathen . . . Wherefore the Lord brought upon them the captains of the host of the king of Assyria . . .' (*2 Chronicles 33.9* and *11*).

This inscribed baked clay prism of Esarhaddon describes his invasion, naming Manasseh.

ASSYRIAN QUOTE

'I called up the kings of the Hatti land and of the regions on the other side of the river *[Euphrates]*: Ba'lu, King of Tyre, Manasseh, King of Judah *[plus 20 other named rulers]* all these I sent out and made them transport under terrible difficulties to Nineveh . . . building materials for my palace: large logs, long beams, boards of cedar and pine . . . and from their quarries in the mountains statues of deities made of stone . . . slabs of limestone, asnan stone, large and small grained breccia.'

At a later stage Manasseh was taken into captivity by Esarhaddon's son.

Courtesy: University of Pennsylvania Museum, USA.

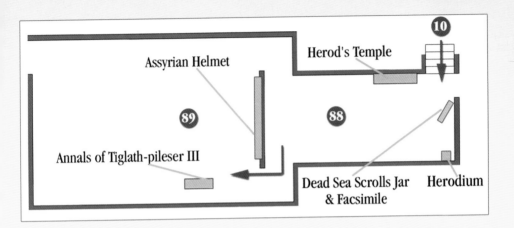

At this point we take a brief detour down the stairs by the relief of Sargon II
and Sennacherib to Rooms 88 and 89, where several items of interest are
shown, one of which (*Annals of Tiglath-pileser III*) is direct evidence.

Dead Sea Scrolls and the Temple 200 BC

Room 88 – Archaeology of the New Testament

'A pottery lidded jar of the sort used to store the Dead Sea Scrolls'

(With a facsimile of part of a leather scroll recording an internal dispute within
the Dead Sea Community, but like a scripture scroll in appearance.)

This jar was found at the site of the Essene community monastery,
eleven caves from where the scrolls were found and retrieved in
1947-1956. Thousands of portions of Old Testament books (including all except *Esther*), some written as long ago as 200 BC, have
established the accuracy of the Masoretic Hebrew manuscripts of
later centuries. Seventeen copies of *Isaiah* were found, one being a
leather scroll 24 feet long and 10 inches wide, made from 17 sheets
sewn together. Over the centuries since hardly anything has changed
providing stunning proof of the extraordinary preservation of the
Bible.

Room 88 – Archaeology of the New Testament

Left: Dead Sea Scrolls Jar [WA 131444] in Room 88.

Above: Facsimile of a typical scroll portion, in this case not a Scripture, in Room 88.

A Magnificent Scale Model of Herod's Temple

Also in this room is a model of the Temple at the time of Christ. (Smaller, commercially produced copies of this are becoming familiar objects even seen in homes these days.) This is the work of the Rev Johann Tenz, an Anglican clergyman, who worked in the late nineteenth century, basing his model on his enormous knowledge and on major excavations at the time.

When the Lord Jesus Christ came to Jerusalem, Herod the Great's Temple had just been constructed on an expanded area of 35 acres. It was the 'largest sacred compound in the ancient world'. Pillars of white marble made from single stones (37½ feet tall) enclosed the courtyard. Gentiles were excluded from all except the outer court on

pain of death (see *Temple Notice* on page 121). Today, only the Wailing Wall survives of the walls. The cornerstone was revealed by archaeologists in 1967. This is the Temple that was destroyed in AD 70, an eyewitness account being left by the Jewish historian Josephus. The Herodium, Herod's hilltop fortress, built 40 BC near Bethlehem, is also the subject of a model.

Walk into Room 89 – Assyrian Art and look for a wall case just as you enter the gallery containing an 8th-century BC Assyrian iron helmet (from Nimrud). One can imagine this being worn by a soldier at the invasion of Hezekiah's Judah.

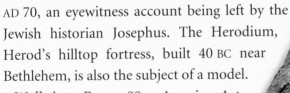

Assyrian iron helmet with bronze inlay
c. 8th century BC [WA 22496] in Room 89.

Annals of Tiglath-pileser III

In a case on the left as you enter Room 89 is another key corroboration of Bible history. This is part of a clay tablet record left by Tiglath-pileser III which includes information about his attack (734-732 BC) on a number of kings – of Judah, Ammon, Moab, Ashkelon, Edom, Gaza, and Tyre. The story of this attack is on page 24. This tablet confirms yet again the record of *2 Kings 15.29*, which tells of how the Assyrian king took districts of Israel, Judah and other territories, and deported many inhabitants to Assyria. (This was in the time of Ahaz, Pekah and Rezin.)

The Annals of Tiglath-pileser III soundly corroborate several
passages of the Bible in describing his invasion of Israel (at the time
of King Pekah) and his defeat of Rezin, king of Syria [WA K 3751], Room 89.

Human-
headed
Winged
Bull

Nineveh Palace Reliefs

West
Stairs

Tirhakah

Tiglath-
pileser
III

Chariot of
Tiglath-pileser III

Nineveh Palace Reliefs

We retrace our steps to Room 8 and proceed past the Chariot of Tiglath-pileser III into Room 9. [If closed, continue to Room 4.]

This gallery called 'Nineveh Palace Reliefs' contains stone reliefs from the two sides of a courtyard of Sennacherib's south-west palace at Nineveh. Among these reliefs we see (two-thirds of the way down on the right) the much photographed picture of a Phoenician ship or 'ship of Tarshish'. Such a ship did not necessarily come from Tarshish, which may have been a distant Mediterranean place (possibly a port in Spain). The term described any 'ocean-going galley or man-of-war, with a long prow for ramming' (R. D. Barnett). Such

Ship of Tarshish [WA 124772], in Room 9

Above: Campaigning in Southern Iraq 640-620 BC – The Assyrian king watches as prisoners are brought in and heads and booty are piled up in a palmgrove [WA 124825], in Room 9. The brutality of Assyria brought terror to Judah also.

Below: Attack on the town of Alammu c. 700-692 BC – Archers shoot at the town and spearmen work their way towards the walls. The name of the town was written above but only the end of it survives [WA 124785], in Room 9.

ships are referred to several times in the Bible. Most famously, Jonah boarded a ship going to Tarshish. The scenes here chiefly show the transferring of the human-headed bulls of the palace doors from the quarries where they were fashioned.

At the end of the gallery on the left is a war scene, full of fear and tension, showing archers and siege troops poised to attack a city – but not Jerusalem as sometimes suggested.

The evidence of burning is also to be seen here, for Nineveh fell in 612 BC, as Nahum had predicted (at some time during the preceding fifty years), by fire and flood. 'Fire shall devour thee,' said Nahum. He also said that the gates of the rivers would be opened so that the palaces would be dissolved. When the Babylonians took the city they set fire to it and caused the Khoser River to flood the palace.

If this gallery is closed, head along Room 4 (the Egyptian Sculpture Gallery) towards the West Stairs, pausing only to glance at the *Ram of Tirhakah*. Taharqa is the alternative spelling. (See map on page 47.) Ignore the pharaohs for the moment. Tirhakah was the

Ethiopian king-regent who marched north to fight against Assyria at the very time Sennacherib laid siege to Lachish *(2 Kings 19.9* and *Isaiah 37.9).* Sennacherib was distracted, left Judah to counter the threat, and returned to have his army destroyed by the angel of the Lord. Tirhakah later became king of Egypt during the Ethiopian Dynasty. He is to be seen on this statue positioned between the front legs of his god – a ram.

King Tirhakah, 690-640 BC
[EA 1779]

Room 4 – Egyptian Sculpture

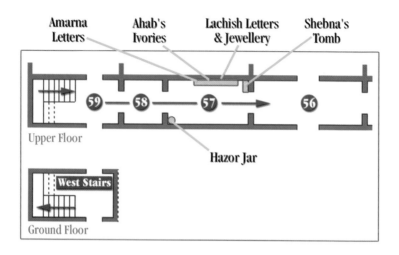

Amarna Letters — Ahab's Ivories — Lachish Letters & Jewellery — Shebna's Tomb

59 — 58 — 57 → 56

Upper Floor

Hazor Jar

West Stairs

Ground Floor

Canaanite storage jar from Hazor used for storing grain or liquid, 14th century BC [WA 132309], in Room 57.

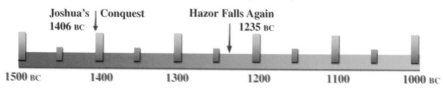

JUDGES, DEBORAH (BARAK)

Joshua's 1406 BC | Conquest

Hazor Falls Again 1235 BC

1500 BC   1400   1300   1200   1100   1000 BC

Whether we have come through Room 9 or Room 4 we now climb the West Stairs to the upper level and proceed straight ahead through Rooms 59 and 58 into Room 57, the Raymond and Beverly Sackler Gallery of the Ancient Levant. (Levant is the lands of the Middle East bordering the Mediterranean.)

Lift service: from the centre of Room 4, access the Great Court, ask for the West Lift, exit into Room 56 on level 6 and turn left for Room 57.

Joshua's Conquest of Hazor c.1400 BC

On the right-hand side just as you enter Room 57 is a very large storage jar of great significance. It comes from the city of Hazor (Tell el-Qedah) located ten miles north of the Sea of Galilee, the largest Canaanite city prior to Joshua's conquest in 1406 BC. (Excavations indicate 40,000 inhabitants.) This jar, however, was made in the 1300s BC, after Joshua's burning of the city (described in *Joshua 11.10-14*). The likelihood is that this jar (along with other Canaanite pottery of the fourteenth and thirteenth centuries BC, displayed elsewhere in the Museum) shows that the city was re-occupied by the Canaanites, as the Bible says. Certainly Joshua did not occupy it, but left it abandoned. *Joshua 11.13* says that defeated cities 'stood still on their mounds' (the literal Hebrew).

The Canaanite re-occupation lasted until the time of the Judges, when (in 1235 BC) Deborah and Barak took back the region and the city (recorded in *Judges 4-5*). In the 1950s, excavations at Hazor by Prof Yigael Yadin found signs of violent destruction and abandonment in the 1200s BC, as well as easily datable pottery. The Canaanite re-occupation had clearly come to an end. A two-fold conquest of Hazor by Israelites, with around 160 years of resumed Canaanite occupation in between, would fit these findings.

THESE PAGES

DATES
1400–1235 BC

CHIEF PEOPLE
Joshua
Deborah
Barak

BOOKS OF BIBLE
Joshua 11.10-14
Judges 4–5

THESE PAGES

DATES
From 1390 BC

CHIEF PEOPLE
Amenophis III & IV
Canaanite kinglets
Joshua

BOOKS OF BIBLE
Joshua 12.9-24

Canaanite Rulers Plead for Help Against the 'Apiru

From 1390 BC

The Amarna Letters and Joshua's Troops

Crossing to the left wall of Room 57, we find several magnificent artefacts confirming Bible history. The first of these are several *Amarna Letters* displayed in Case 8. In 1887 a store of 382 ancient letters was discovered in Egypt at the site of Tell el-Amarna. These clay tablets had been written to two pharaohs (Amenophis III and IV) over a period from 1390 BC. The senders were officials and 'kinglets' of the Canaanite cities of Palestine about the time that Joshua and the children of Israel were settling in the land. Palestine was then part of the Egyptian empire.

Soon after 1380 BC Amenophis IV (also spelled Amenhotep) moved the Egyptian capital, together with the 'Foreign Office' files relating to his father's reign, from Thebes to Amarna.

Many of the letters refer to impending invasions and hostilities by the 'Apiru (and by another group which is thought to be a code logogram for the same people). In all probability the 'Apiru were not strictly the Israelites but a marauding nomadic people who had been in Canaan before the arrival of the Israelites. But to the Canaanites, the Israelites were the same as the 'Apiru, this having become a pejorative term for any unsettled and hostile group. Conservative scholars, therefore, equate the 'Apiru with the Israelites who had by this time arrived in the land, had completed their initial conquests, and were taking other cities.

The governor of Jerusalem wrote several letters to pharaoh,

Letters 3 & 4 refer to the 'Apiru, most probably the Israelites.

Letter 4 (left):
From Biridiya, king of Megiddo who accuses the king of Acco of treachery by releasing the captured 'Apiru leader Labayu instead of sending him to Egypt [Case 8 – EA 29855], in Room 57.

Letter 3 (right):
From Yapahu, king of Gezer who begs pharaoh for help in defending his city against raids by the 'Apiru [Case 8 – EA 29832], in Room 57.

He writes:
'Because the 'Apiru are stronger than we are, may the king, my lord, help me to escape from the 'Apiru, that the 'Apiru do not destroy us.'

pleading for help to resist these invaders. In one he cries –

> 'The 'Apiru plunder all the lands of the king. If archers are here this year then the lands of the king, my lord, will remain. But if the archers are not here, then the lands of the king, my lord, are lost . . . All the lands of the king, my lord, are going to ruin.'

Pharaoh Amenophis made no response to such appeals, not being greatly interested in his Palestine possessions. According to the dating information of the Bible, Joshua entered the Promised Land around 1406 BC. The *Amarna Letters* tell us about the state of Palestine *after* the entry of Joshua into the land, not *before* it. The book of *Joshua* refers to 31 independent city-states that had their own kings (*Joshua 12.9-24*). As Dr John J. Davis points out:

> 'The success of Israel brought about the end of many of the independent states, thus leaving only a few self-sufficient political entities in southern Canaan.'

The *Amarna Letters* confirm this picture of Joshua's work, for they reflect the survival of only *four* independent city-states with their own kings. Even if the marauding 'Apiru were not the Israelites, the *Amarna Letters* certainly testify to the *results* of Joshua's conquest as recorded in the Bible. If the 'Apiru were other than the Israelites, they subsequently vanished from history startlingly quickly, which is barely credible.

Letter 1: From the king of Hazor who tells pharaoh that he is loyal and is keeping his cities [EA 29831], in Room 57.

The Stela of Merneptah (Or 'Israel Stele')

This 7½ foot tall basalt stela carries the earliest mention of Israel outside Scripture. Pharaoh Merneptah (1236-1223 BC) mounted a campaign to Canaan about 1231 BC (in the time of the Judges). Here he claims: 'Israel is laid waste, bare of seed.' This inscription shows that Israel as an ethnic group was well settled in Canaan by this time. Merneptah's invasion (possibly at the time of Deborah and Barak) is not mentioned in the Bible, and is thought to have affected only the Jezreel area, if carried out at all. There are many vain boasts in Egyptian records, but the testimony to Israel's known existence in the land of Canaan is clear. Discovered in 1896 in Merneptah's mortuary at Thebes, it is now in the Cairo Museum.

This famous and highly significant monument cannot be viewed on our tour, but we mention it here, alongside the *Amarna Letters*, as it confirms the settlement of the Israelites in the land of Canaan, in accordance with the books of *Exodus, Joshua* and *Judges.*

Top portion of the Stela of Merneptah. The reference to Israel is lower down, out of this photograph. (In the Cairo Museum)

'Ahab's Ivories' 874–853 BC

BIBLE QUOTE

'Now the rest of the acts of Ahab, and all that he did, and the ivory house which he made, and all the cities that he built, are they not written in the book of the chronicles of the kings of Israel?' (1 Kings 22.39.)

Displayed in wall case 10 of the Gallery of the Ancient Levant is a panel bearing several pieces of carved ivory found in 1931-35 at Ahab's royal palace in Samaria, although whether these particular examples were made for him or a successor is uncertain. Amos said that God would destroy 'the houses of ivory' and condemned those who 'lie upon beds of ivory' *(Amos 3.15, 6.4)*. Ahab's 'ivory house' at Samaria was so called because of the carved and inlaid ivory friezes and embellishments throughout the palace. The craftsmen were Phoenician, and the ivory came from Syrian elephants. Some entire walls were covered with carved ivory panelling, while similar ornamentation decorated the furniture. Ahab's wife Jezebel, a Phoenician princess from Tyre, would have revelled in this as Ahab lavished such excesses upon his royal buildings.

THESE PAGES
DATES
874–853 BC
CHIEF PEOPLE
Ahab
Jezebel
Amos
AT THE TIME OF
Elijah
BOOKS OF BIBLE
1 Kings 22.39
Amos 3.15; 6.4

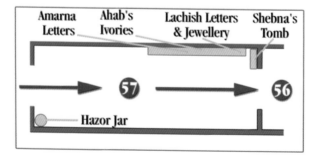

Amarna Letters — Ahab's Ivories — Lachish Letters & Jewellery — Shebna's Tomb — 57 — 56 — Hazor Jar

Room 57 – The Ancient Levant

Phoenician ivories from Samaria, around
9th century BC [Case 10 – WA L 31-48],
in Room 57.

Military Communications as Nebuchadnezzar Closes In, 586 BC

The Lachish Letters – confirming the state of impending doom described by Jeremiah

THESE PAGES
DATES
586 BC
CHIEF PEOPLE
Nebuchadnezzar
Jeremiah
Zedekiah, king of Judah
AT THE TIME OF
Daniel
Ezekiel
BOOKS OF BIBLE
Jeremiah 34.6-7; 38.4; 42.1

These letters (in Case 10) take us back to 586 BC when Nebuchadnezzar, king of Babylon, invaded Judah, destroying Jerusalem and its Temple with great violence, and carrying multitudes into captivity. At the time the prophet Jeremiah was in Jerusalem warning King Zedekiah of the impending catastrophe. Near to Jerusalem was the fortress town of Lachish (destroyed by Sennacherib over a century before, but later rebuilt). These letters were found in 1935 in the ruins of a guardroom by the main gate of Lachish. Twenty-one letters were found, written in joined-up writing, in black ink on pieces of broken pottery (called ostraca). Written in alphabetic Hebrew, they are urgent messages, full of 'eleventh hour' tension, written as Nebuchadnezzar's army closed in on a very apprehensive Jerusalem.

The writer was Hosha'yahu (Hoshaiah), the commander of a military outpost or small town garrison. He wrote to the Lachish military governor, whose name was Ya'osh. One letter appears to have been written shortly after the state of affairs described in *Jeremiah 34.6-7*, which mentions that Jeremiah delivered a message to King Zedekiah while the cities of Lachish and Azekah still remained standing. The relevant Lachish letter in our picture reads:

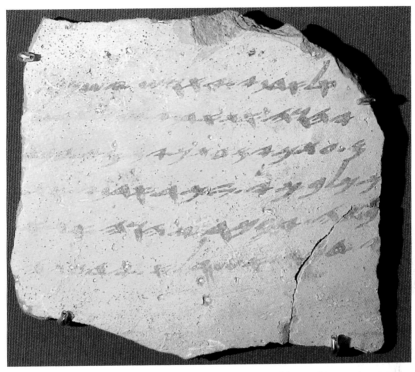

One of the Lachish Letters [Case 10 – WA 125702] in Room 57 quoted in our description below. More are pictured next page.

'May Yahweh cause my lord to hear this very day tidings of good. And now, in accordance with everything my lord has written, so has your servant done. I have written on the door everything which my lord has written to me . . . and I report that we are watching for the fire signals of Lachish according to the directions which my lord has given, because we cannot see Azekah.'

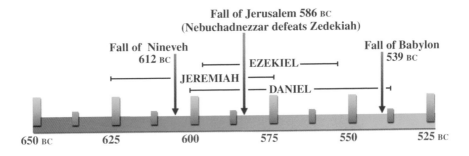

Fall of Jerusalem 586 BC
(Nebuchadnezzar defeats Zedekiah)

Fall of Nineveh
612 BC

Fall of Babylon
539 BC

EZEKIEL

JEREMIAH

DANIEL

650 BC   625   600   575   550   525 BC

It is possible that Azekah had fallen. Another Lachish letter logs the departure of a deputation to Egypt, and also includes the following:

LACHISH QUOTE

> 'And as for the letter of Tobiah, servant of the king, which came to Shallum son of Jaddua through the prophet, saying, "Beware!" thy servant hath sent it to my lord.'

Who was the prophet referred to here? It is likely to have been Jeremiah. (This is the first known mention of a Jewish prophet outside the Bible.) In another letter the complaint is made that:

LACHISH QUOTE

> 'The words of the princes are not good, but they weaken our hands and slacken the hands of those who hear about them.'

This was the very charge which the princes made against Jeremiah when they demanded his execution – 'let this man be put to death: for thus he weakeneth the hands of the men of war' (*Jeremiah 38.4*). Hoshaiah the outpost commander was clearly in sympathy with Jeremiah in seeing that the policy of the princes, relying on Egypt, would bring certain defeat and devastation.

Many biblical names appear on these letters. Hosha'yahu appears in *Jeremiah 42.1* as Hoshaiah. Ya'osh means Josiah. Neriah, Gemariah and Shemaiah are also names which occur both in the *Lachish Letters* and the book of *Jeremiah* (Shemaiah occurs six times in *Jeremiah*). It is not likely that these people, bearing common names, were the same as those mentioned in *Jeremiah*, but the *Lachish*

One of the Lachish Letters [Case 10, WA 125701] in Room 57.

Room 57 – The Ancient Levant

Lachish Letters [Case 10 – WA 125703-7, 125715a] in Room 57.

Letters obviously relate to the crisis leading to the fall of Jerusalem, confirming powerfully the historical reality of the biblical record, including the situation in the city reflected in the book of the prophet *Jeremiah*.

Jeremiah the Prophet

In one of the most graphic books in the Bible, Jeremiah warns and pleads with people to seek their individual, spiritual salvation, as the land would fall. No prophet uses more illustrations in his preaching. With great feeling he reasons with individuals to seek and find God in a personal way. He predicts the coming of Christ, who would be divine, and who would make a way of forgiveness for all who trust in Him. Jeremiah calls Christ – 'The Lord our righteousness', referring to our need of a Saviour who would take on our behalf the punishment of our sin, and offer His own perfect righteousness to make us acceptable to God. The prophet also accurately predicted the 70-year captivity of the Jews in Babylon, and the detailed future of other nations – all of which has taken place.

The Inscription over Shebna's Tomb [WA 125205], in Room 57

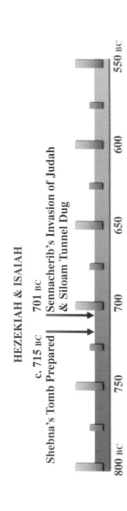

HEZEKIAH & ISAIAH

c. 715 BC   701 BC

Shebna's Tomb Prepared   Sennacherib's Invasion of Judah
& Siloam Tunnel Dug

800 BC   750   700   650   600   550 BC

The Noble Tomb for Which Shebna Was Denounced by Isaiah c. 715 BC

Set on the wall, above head height, to the left of the door leading to Room 56.

This inscription on a slab of stone was found over 100 years ago near Jerusalem, but the inscription was only translated in the 1950s. It was taken from above the door of a burial chamber cut out of the solid rock of a hillside. The person for whom this tomb was prepared was most probably the Shebna denounced by the prophet Isaiah. Chancellor in Hezekiah's early administration, he was later deposed from office, and finally captured by the Assyrians. The inscription reads:

HEBREW QUOTE

'This is _____yahu, who is Over the House. There is no silver and gold here; only [him] and the bones of his slave-wife. Cursed be the man who opens this.'

The partly obscured name is doubtless 'Shebanyahu' or Shebna. 'Over the House' is a term for the controller of the royal revenues. Shebna was denounced by Isaiah for preparing a splendid tomb for himself, a mark of his arrogance and self-enrichment. In *Isaiah 22.15-17* we read:

BIBLE QUOTE

'Thus saith the Lord God of hosts, Go, get thee unto this treasurer, even unto Shebna, which is over the house, and say, What hast thou here? and whom hast thou here, that thou hast hewed thee out a sepulchre here, as he that heweth him out a sepulchre on high, and that graveth an habitation for himself in a rock? Behold, the Lord will carry thee away with a mighty captivity.'

Shebna was duly deposed from office and replaced by Eliakim the son of Hilkiah just as Isaiah said. By the time Sennacherib came to invade Judah, Eliakim was in office and heading up the negotiating team sent to meet the Assyrian chief of staff *(Isaiah 36.3* and *37.2).*

It is possible that the disgraced Shebna was seized during this invasion. Perhaps he moved to an area which the Assyrians overran. (He is not the same person as 'Shebna the scribe' who helped Eliakim.) At any rate, if Isaiah's prediction is rightly understood, Shebna was 'tossed like a ball into a large country' where he died *(Isaiah 22.17-18)* so that he never actually occupied his upper-class tomb. The inscription was presumptuous, and in it he claims he is innocent of Isaiah's charge. This may be the same Shebna whose limestone seal (from Lachish) is also in Case 10 below the *Lachish Letters* [WA 1980 . . . 12011], bearing his name and also that of his father Ahab, though obviously not the earlier king.

A Further Confirmation of Biblical Information from Isaiah's Time

The name of Sargon II (king of Assyria 722-705 BC) was unknown outside the Bible until his palace at Khorsabad was discovered in 1843 by a brilliant French diplomat and archaeologist. *Isaiah 20.1* tells how Sargon sent his 'Tartan' (his commander-in-chief) to capture Ashdod (in 711 BC). The biblical information was exactly confirmed by the inscription on fragments of a basalt stela (of Sargon) found at Ashdod in 1963 (now in the Israel Museum in Jerusalem). Sargon left to posterity the following claim:

ASSYRIAN QUOTE

'Azuri king of Ashdod had schemed not to deliver tribute . . . I marched . . . besieged and conquered his cities . . . and they bore my yoke.'

We have already seen Sargon's larger than life picture in stone, and other items from his Khorsabad palace. In Room 55, ahead, there is a unique glass jar [WA 90952] bearing a cuneiform inscription – 'Palace of Sargon, King of Assyria'. (This will be found in Case 8 for more leisurely browsers.) One after another the alleged 'mythical figures' of the Bible have been revealed as true people by the archaeologist's spade.

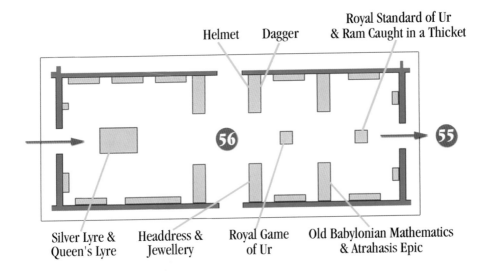

Helmet   Dagger   Royal Standard of Ur & Ram Caught in a Thicket

56   **55**

Silver Lyre & Queen's Lyre   Headdress & Jewellery   Royal Game of Ur   Old Babylonian Mathematics & Atrahasis Epic

The Royal Tombs of Ur c. 2500 BC

THESE PAGES

DATE
c. 2500 BC

CHIEF PEOPLE
Abraham

BOOKS OF BIBLE
Genesis 11.31

We proceed into Room 56, the Raymond and Beverly Sackler Gallery of Early Mesopotamia.

This is the 'home' of artefacts from the Royal Tombs at Ur (around 2500 BC). Excavations at Ur (pictured overleaf) were carried out by Sir Leonard Woolley between 1922 and 1934, the city having been discovered in 1854. The very existence of Ur was denied by critics of the Bible prior to its discovery. In the materials from these excavations there is no direct evidence of the presence of Abraham's family, but they entirely confirm the descriptive language of the *Genesis* record.

The city was clearly an extremely wealthy and sophisticated place, and the Royal Tombs of Ur have yielded up magnificent treasures. According to the Bible, Abraham grew up in or outside the city during the 22nd century BC. The Ur excavations centred on the great Ziggurat (a temple to the moon god) shown in the photograph. The city had two-storeyed houses, main drainage, and a commercial system based on written contracts, money, receipts and similar tokens of a trading system. The exhibits in this room help us to appreciate the kind of advanced but idolatrous civilisation out of which

Above: Excavations at Ur, showing the Ziggurat; Inset: Sir Leonard Woolley
Below: Artist's impression of a Mesopotamian Ziggurat about 550 BC, in Room 55

Abraham was called by God. Several beautiful objects of art also illustrate the authenticity of biblical descriptions, although they pre-date the time of Abraham.

The depiction of an army or, as it used to be thought, a wealthy family on the move, helps us picture the long journey of Abraham and his family (see illustration overleaf – *Royal Standard of Ur*). The army is on one side and the booty parade on the other. The statuette of a ram made of gold, silver, lapis and shell, depicts 'a ram caught in a thicket'. Two like this were discovered. For this to have been the subject of an artist shows that this situation was not so rare. Once again, the statue pre-dates the offering of Isaac, but helps to authenticate the narrative. Around the room are displayed many other interesting items from the Abrahamic period.

The Royal Tombs contained the famous *Queen's Lyre* [Case 9 – WA 121198A], a reconstruction of which is on display here. There are impressive items of literature, advanced mathematics, and science, and evidence of widespread literacy among the people. (A recipe for glass is displayed in Room 55 [Case 5 – WA 120960], from which Pilkington's once successfully made small cups.) The exhibits help the viewer to appreciate the advanced culture of Ur, and the great test of faith for Abraham when he left (in all probability) a secure house, forsook all and set out for the land which God would show him. Also in Room 56 is a Babylonian flood story the *Atrahasis Epic* from 1630 BC [Case 25 – WA 78941], but we comment more fully on the Babylonian creation and flood tablets in Room 55 (pages 85-88).

Jacob
Enters Egypt
1876 BC

Abraham Leaves
Ur 2091 BC

The Exodus
1446 BC

3000 BC   2500   2000   1500   1000 BC

Room 56 – Early Mesopotamia

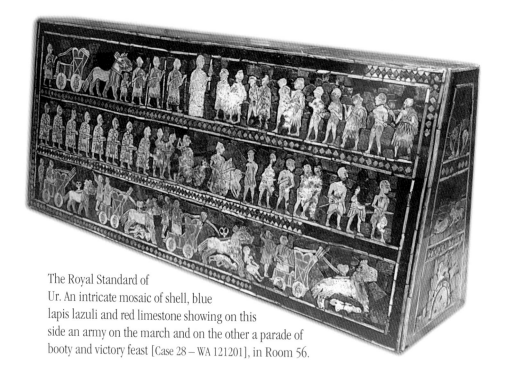

The Royal Standard of
Ur. An intricate mosaic of shell, blue
lapis lazuli and red limestone showing on this
side an army on the march and on the other a parade of
booty and victory feast [Case 28 – WA 121201], in Room 56.

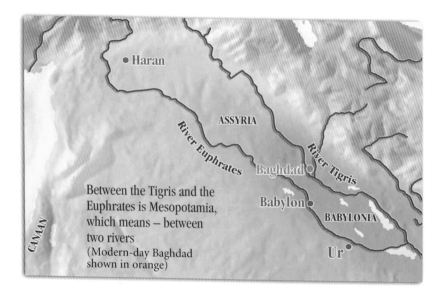

Between the Tigris and the
Euphrates is Mesopotamia,
which means – between
two rivers
(Modern-day Baghdad
shown in orange)

The Ram Caught in a Thicket, crafted several centuries before
Abraham [Case 28 – WA 122200], in Room 56.

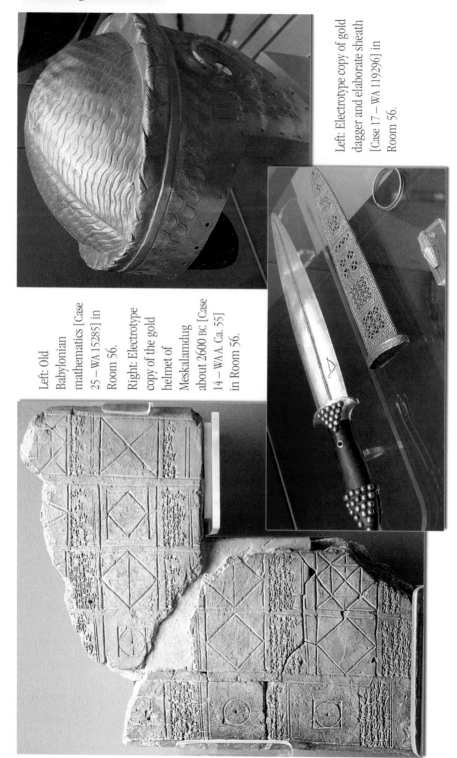

Left: Electrotype copy of gold dagger and elaborate sheath [Case 17 – WA 119296] in Room 56.

Left: Old Babylonian mathematics [Case 25 – WA 15285] in Room 56.

Right: Electrotype copy of the gold helmet of Meskalamdug about 2600 BC [Case 14 – WA.A. Ca. 55] in Room 56.

Reconstructed headdress of a Sumerian woman with jewellery found on bodies,
c. 2600 BC [Case 12 – WA 122302, 122306-15, 122317-18, 122318 A, 1224113], in Room 56.

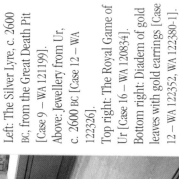

Left: The Silver Lyre, c. 2600 BC, from the Great Death Pit [Case 9 – WA 121199].

Above: Jewellery from Ur, c. 2600 BC [Case 12 – WA 122326].

Top right: The Royal Game of Ur [Case 16 – WA 120834].

Bottom right: Diadem of gold leaves with gold earrings [Case 12 – WA 122352, WA 122380-1].

All items in Room 56.

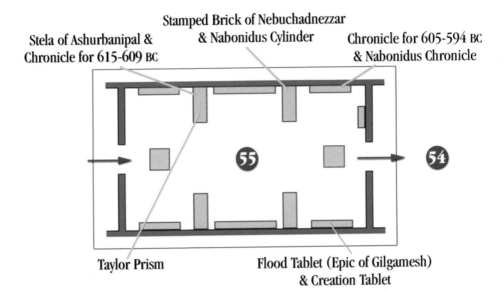

Stamped Brick of Nebuchadnezzar
& Nabonidus Cylinder

Stela of Ashurbanipal &
Chronicle for 615-609 BC

Chronicle for 605-594 BC
& Nabonidus Chronicle

Taylor Prism

Flood Tablet (Epic of Gilgamesh)
& Creation Tablet

Further Direct Corroboration of Bible History

Entering Room 55 (Later Mesopotamia) we look at a wealth of tablets giving another section of solid evidence for the historical accuracy of the Bible.

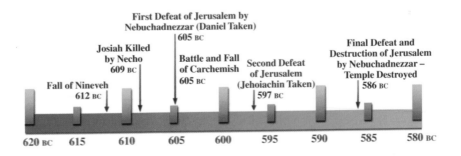

First Defeat of Jerusalem by
Nebuchadnezzar (Daniel Taken)
605 BC

Josiah Killed
by Necho
609 BC

Battle and Fall
of Carchemish
605 BC

Second Defeat
of Jerusalem
(Jehoiachin Taken)
597 BC

Final Defeat and
Destruction of Jerusalem
by Nebuchadnezzar –
Temple Destroyed
586 BC

Fall of Nineveh
612 BC

620 BC   615   610   605   600   595   590   585   580 BC

Room 55 – Later Mesopotamia

The Taylor Prism
[Case 11 – WA 91032]
in Room 55

The Taylor Prism is named after its first owner, Colonel R. Taylor, who found it at Nineveh in 1830. Inscribed in cuneiform script in 691 BC, it is the final edition of Sennacherib's annals. (A similar prism bearing the same record is held by Chicago University.) The king's final eight military campaigns are described.

Sennacherib reports his (701 BC) defeat of the Phoenicians at Tyre and Sidon; his march south taking tribute from Ammon, Moab, Edom and Ashdod; his replacing of a rebellious ruler at Ashkelon, and his defeat of an Egyptian army on its way to assist Palestine.

The king's besieging of 46 Judean cities is reported together with his deportation of 200,150 Judeans, and also his claim to have laid siege to Jerusalem, although the Bible says he did not do so. Sennacherib very strangely omits any mention of the outcome of the siege, and claims no victory. The record describes the tribute paid by Hezekiah, broadly agreeing with the biblical amount, but Sennacherib is silent about the loss of his army.

The Taylor Prism

In the first protruding case on the left in Room 55 we may view the *Taylor Prism* 691 BC. Referred to on page 37, this is the definitive last record of Sennacherib, including his version of his 701 BC campaign against Hezekiah in Judah. However, this six-sided baked clay prism does not actually refer to Lachish, nor does Sennacherib care to record the destruction of his army.

In this same case are two *Stelae of Ashurbanipal* (king of Assyria 668-627 BC), who deported to Babylon Manasseh, Hezekiah's son, leading to his repentance and restoration to kingship in Jerusalem *(2 Chronicles 33.10-13)*. See also page 42.

The Remarkable Babylonian Chronicles

Among the most impressive items in the Museum verifying Bible history are the sensational *Babylonian Chronicles*, the records of the Babylonian kings who took the mantle of empire after the collapse of Assyria. Covering the period from 615 to 539 BC, these inscribed clay tablets substantiate many events. They provide details of the accessions and deaths of Babylonian kings, together with the main events in each year of their reign. In Case 11 is the *Babylonian Chronicle* for the period 615 to 609 BC, pictured and described on the coming pages.

The Babylonian Chronicle for 615-609 BC

Report of the Fall of Nineveh – 612 BC

The *Babylonian Chronicle* for 615-609 BC confirms the collapse of the Assyrian empire and the fall of Nineveh, its mighty capital city, to the Babylonians. In the Bible, Nahum and Zephaniah had predicted the fall of Nineveh, and Jeremiah recorded it.

Impregnable and powerful though it seemed, Nahum described the city's coming humiliation and devastation, referring particularly to massacre and devouring fire (the evidence of which we have already seen on other Assyrian sculptures).

This *Babylonian Chronicle* tells how the Babylonians (with their allies) attacked Nineveh in 612 BC. It includes the following sentences –

'The king of Akkad *[Nabopolassar of Babylon]* called out his army . . . the king of Umman-manda *[Medes or Scythians]* crossed and marched along the bank of the river Tigris and camped against Nineveh . . . A great attack they mounted . . . a great defeat of this dominant people was made . . . great spoil of the city and temple they carried away and the city was reduced to a mount of ruin and heaps of debris.'

The presence of Egyptian troops in the Euphrates region in 609 BC (referred to in *2 Kings 23.29* and also *2 Chronicles 35.20-24*) is also confirmed by this chronicle. The *2 Kings* verse says –

'In his days Pharaoh-nechoh king of Egypt went up against *[this should read "alongside"]* the king of Assyria to the river Euphrates: and king Josiah went against him.'

Josiah, one of the best kings of Judah, here made a fatal mistake. After the fall of Nineveh, Egypt went to the aid of the crumbling Assyrians, and Josiah, contrary to all warnings, got involved and led

Chronicle for 615-609 BC
[Case 11 – WA 21901] in
Room 55

THESE PAGES

DATES
615–609 BC

CHIEF PEOPLE
Nabopolassar
Pharaoh Nechoh
Josiah, king of Judah

AT THE TIME OF
Jeremiah

BOOKS OF BIBLE
Nahum
Zephaniah
2 Kings 23.29
2 Chronicles 35.20-24

his army to Megiddo, where Pharaoh Nechoh killed him.

The *Babylonian Chronicle* covering the year 609 BC confirms the Egyptian presence in the region at this time when there was a skirmish for the city of Harran (where the Assyrian king had fled after the fall of Nineveh). The chronicle says –

BABYLONIAN QUOTE

'In the month Iyyou of his sixteenth year . . . *[Nabopolassar of Babylon]* called out his army and marched to Assyria . . . and marched after Ashur-uballit *[king of Assyria]* to Harran. Fear . . . fell on him and on the army of Egypt which had come to his help . . . they abandoned the city.'

Nebuchadnezzar Confirms the Bible – Two Attacks on Jerusalem 605 & 597 BC

Babylonian Chronicle for 605-594 BC

The chronicle for the first eleven years of Nebuchadnezzar's reign (605-594 BC) confirms the biblical record of the battle of Carchemish and the siege of Jerusalem.

The Bible says that in the fourth year of Jehoiakim, Josiah's son (605 BC), Pharaoh Nechoh came again to help the dying Assyrian empire withstand the Babylonians (*Jeremiah 46* refers). Jeremiah had previously prophesied that Nebuchadnezzar would win all his battles against Assyria and Egypt and would then take Judah into captivity for 70 years (*Jeremiah 25.9-11; 27.6-11*).

When the Egyptian army clashed with the Babylonian army under the generalship of crown prince Nebuchadnezzar, the result was the slaughter of the Egyptians at Carchemish (*Jeremiah 46*).

At this time Nebuchadnezzar also besieged Jerusalem (*Daniel 1.1-5* and *2 Chronicles 36.6*). He had put King Jehoiakim in fetters in preparation for transportation to Babylon. As *2 Kings 24.1* shows, he had second thoughts and decided to leave him in charge at Jerusalem as a puppet king. He did, however, take some prisoners, including the young man Daniel and his friends, who were selected for special training in Babylon. The *Babylonian Chronicle* broadly confirms these events (without referring to Jehoiakim and the young prisoners). It reads:

THESE PAGES
DATES
605-594 BC
CHIEF PEOPLE
Nebuchadnezzar
Pharaoh Nechoh
Jehoiakim, Jehoiachin &
Zedekiah, kings of Judah
AT THE TIME OF
Jeremiah, Daniel &
Ezekiel
BOOKS OF BIBLE
2 Kings 24.1, 8-17
2 Chronicles 36.6, 9-10
Jeremiah 25, 27
Daniel 1.1-5

BABYLONIAN QUOTE

'In the 21st year the king of Akkad *[Nabopolassar]* stayed in his own land, Nebuchadnezzar his eldest son, the crown prince, mustered and took command of the troops. He marched to Carchemish . . . against the Egyptian army . . . accomplished their defeat and beat them to non-existence. As for the rest . . . which escaped . . . the Babylonian troops overtook and defeated them. At that time Nebuchadnezzar conquered the whole area of the Hatti country.'

The 'Hatti country' included Palestine, thus endorsing the biblical statement that Jerusalem was besieged and annexed in 605 BC.

Chronicle for 605-594 BC [Case 15 – WA 21946] in Room 55

This same *Babylonian Chronicle* continues to vindicate the biblical record right down to the minute chronological details. Two passages of Scripture, *2 Kings 24.8-17* and *2 Chronicles 36.9-10*, describe how Nebuchadnezzar again besieged Jerusalem in late 598 BC, Jehoiakim dying early in the siege. His eighteen-year-old son Jehoiachin ruled only three months and ten days and was forced to surrender. The Babylonians entered the city in March, 597 BC, and took great treasures, carrying away King Jehoiachin, together with 10,000 other captives including all the skilled men and soldiers, leaving only the poorest people and appointing another puppet king (Jehoiachin's uncle, Zedekiah). The *Babylonian Chronicle* bears this out, saying:

> **BABYLONIAN QUOTE** 'The king of Akkad mustered his troops, marching to the Hatti-land, and encamped against the city of Judah . . . besieged the city and captured the king. He appointed there a king of his own choice, received its heavy tribute and sent them to Babylon.'

The young Ezekiel was among the captives taken to Babylon.

The biblical statement that King Jehoiachin was deported to Babylon is confirmed by other Babylonian tablets translated in the 1960s which list rations given to prisoners between 595 and 590 BC. Jehoiachin is actually named as being supplied with monthly rations of oil and barley, together with his five sons. Three oil receipts may be dated to 592 BC. The 'ration dockets' are in the Pergamon Museum, Berlin.

There is a long gap in the *Babylonian Chronicle* tablets which have been so far discovered. This gap stretches from 595 to 556 BC and includes the last 33 years of the reign of Nebuchadnezzar. Unfortunately, therefore, the Babylonian records are absent for the year 586 BC, when the puppet king Zedekiah in Jerusalem rebelled, and Nebuchadnezzar's troops were sent for the third time to punish the city, leading to its destruction.

Room 55 – Later Mesopotamia

A Stamped Brick of Nebuchadnezzar 605–562 BC

Nebuchadnezzar reigned over the Babylonian empire from 605 to 562 BC. A mighty conqueror, he was also an outstanding builder, making Babylon the most spectacular city of ancient times *(Daniel 4.30)*. This brick in Case 14 is stamped with the name and titles of Nebuchadnezzar (and of his father). Other bricks of Nebuchadnezzar are seen in Case 12.

A stamped brick of Nebuchadnezzar II (605-562 BC)
[Case 14 – WA 90081] in Room 55

THESE PAGES

DATES
539 BC

CHIEF PEOPLE
Belshazzar
Nabonidus
Cyrus
Daniel

BOOKS OF BIBLE
Daniel 5.5, 30

The Fall of Babylon 539 BC

The acting king of Babylon, Belshazzar, drank and boasted the evening away at a vast feast convened to celebrate Babylonian gods and achievements. *Daniel 5* verses 5 and 30 record –

> BIBLE QUOTE
>
> 'In the same hour came forth fingers of a man's hand, and wrote over against the candlestick upon the plaister of the wall of the king's palace ... In that night was Belshazzar the king of the Chaldeans slain.'

Daniel gives an account of the events in the Babylonian palace just before the Medes seized and occupied the city, taking over its empire in the year 539 BC. Belshazzar is named as the feasting king who promised Daniel that he would be the third ruler in the kingdom if he could interpret the writing on the wall.

Before the mid-1800s many scholars claimed that this was sheer fiction on the part of the Bible, because the last king of Babylon was known to be Nabonidus, and the name 'Belshazzar' was unheard of outside the book of *Daniel*. Even Herodotus, the Greek historian who wrote up the history of Babylon in 450 BC, had evidently never heard of Belshazzar. There seemed little hope for the accuracy of the

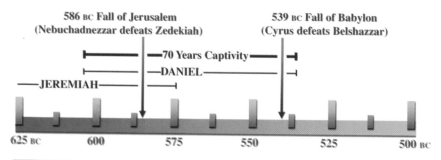

586 BC Fall of Jerusalem
(Nebuchadnezzar defeats Zedekiah)

539 BC Fall of Babylon
(Cyrus defeats Belshazzar)

——70 Years Captivity——

——DANIEL——

——JEREMIAH——

625 BC   600   575   550   525   500 BC

Room 55 – Later Mesopotamia

book of *Daniel*. Inevitably, however, in 1854 Babylonian inscriptions began to yield up their evidence. These tell us that Nabonidus entrusted the kingship to his eldest son while he himself lived in Tema in Arabia.

Cylinder Inscription of Nabonidus

The first invincible item of evidence for Belshazzar is the *Cylinder Inscription of Nabonidus* displayed in Case 14. This was found at the Ziggurat at Ur. It records, in Babylonian cuneiform, how the Ziggurat was reconstructed by Nabonidus. The record ends with a prayer, part of which asks for the religious life of Belshazzar, his son, calling him –

BABYLONIAN QUOTE   'Belsarusur, the firstborn son, the offspring of my heart.'

The Nabonidus Cylinder 555-540 BC [Case 14 – WA 91128] in Room 55

The Nabonidus Chronicle
[Case 15 – WA 35382]
in Room 55

The Nabonidus Chronicle 556–539 BC

The next inscription to see is in Case 15 – exhibit number 26. This chronicle covers the years of Nabonidus from 556 to 539 BC, and says at one point: 'The king was in the city of Tema; the king's son, courtiers and army were in Babylonia.' Daniel's record has therefore been vindicated as truly historical, and we now know why Belshazzar (as co-regent) could only offer Daniel the 'third place' in the kingdom.

Nabonidus spent ten years in Tema. His chronicle confirms the historic fall of Babylon (while Belshazzar ruled) in 539 BC. We read:

BABYLONIAN QUOTE

'The gods of Babylonia entered Babylon from every direction ... when Cyrus attacked the Babylonian army at Opist ... the people of Babylonia revolted ... the troops of Cyrus entered Babylon without battle.'

Room 55 – Later Mesopotamia

Because Daniel made astounding and detailed prophecies in the sixth century BC about the course of future empires up to the time of Christ, critics of the Bible have insisted that the book of *Daniel* was written centuries later. We now have two clear confirmations that the book was written in the sixth century BC.

(1) The author of *Daniel* knew about Belshazzar, whose name had been completely forgotten by 450 BC when Herodotus wrote, and remained unheard of until the archaeological discoveries of our time.

(2) The author also knew that Babylon had been rebuilt by Nebuchadnezzar *(Daniel 4.30)*, another fact that was unknown to later historians until the excavations of more recent times.

The Mesopotamian Legends of Creation and the Flood c. 1800 BC

In Case 10 we view two tablets from the Royal Library at Nineveh, one being part of an ancient Mesopotamian creation story discovered around 1848. The tablet on display is one of seven copied in the seventh century BC from a much older version, thought to have been handed down from around 1800 BC. It calls for comment because cynics have claimed that this ancient epic (along with others) was the source of the *Genesis* account of creation.

In the Mesopotamian story the two original gods Apsu, the male, and Tiamat,

Cuneiform tablet telling the epic of creation
[Case 10 – WA K 3473] in Room 55

the female, are created from water. They then beget all other gods, but these 'children' make so much noise that Apsu is unable to sleep and decides to kill them. However, before he can do so, one of the offspring puts a spell on him and kills him. Tiamat, to avenge his death, takes up the cudgels, but Marduk (another offspring) eliminates her, splitting her in two, and the two parts of her corpse become the heavens and the Earth. Marduk relieves the other gods of all manual work by creating man (from the blood of a defeated giant god), and Marduk then becomes the chief god. Needless to say, none of this has anything in common with the biblical account of creation. Such legends do, however, bear witness to an instinctive human awareness that the universe was created by superior power.

As far as creation is concerned, the Bible says that man was made in the image of one holy and almighty God. Then man disobeyed and lost his spiritual life, becoming a corrupt rebel. The Mesopotamian creation legend, by contrast, is a polytheistic fairyland, full of petty, corrupt, ill-tempered and even vicious gods who are merely a reflection of sinful people, and therefore a human literary creation.

Epic of Gilgamesh Flood Story

The second tablet to be viewed is the *Epic of Gilgamesh* – one of several ancient Mesopotamian flood stories. The tablet is the eleventh of twelve tablets telling the adventures of Gilgamesh, a legendary ruler who searches for immortality. (It is a seventh century BC version, found in the Royal Library of Nineveh.) Once again, biblical cynics claim that the *Genesis* account of Noah's flood was derived from ancient legends such as this. Rather wild remarks have been made to the effect that the *Epic of Gilgamesh* story 'follows the lines of that of Noah closely'. However, as many scholars have pointed out, there are vast differences between the biblical and Mesopotamian accounts of the flood. Indeed, they form absolute 'opposites' in many respects.

Room 55 – Later Mesopotamia

The flood story in the *Gilgamesh Epic* has *some* elements which are similar to the *Genesis* flood, although it must be said that a number of similarities are surely inevitable. To escape a flood, for example, one needs a boat, and to maintain life afterwards, one needs to take animals on board. Accordingly the hero, Utnapishtim, had a boat (a cube 180 feet across) and took some animals with him, though not quite as Noah did. He also took gold and silver – a sure sign of human fiction because he would hardly need such things if his family were to be the sole survivors of a worldwide flood. In the *Genesis* flood, as the waves abated Noah sent out a raven and a dove, while

'The Flood Legend' from the Epic of Gilgamesh, an ancient Babylonian flood story. This is the Assyrian version from Nineveh [Case 10 – WA K 3375], in Room 55.

the *Gilgamesh* boat sends out a dove, swallow and raven.

Overall, however, the accounts are characterised by numerous *dissimilarities* – such as when Utnapishtim offers a sacrifice to the gods which touches off a row between them. The gods of this epic always emerge as materialistic, greedy, violent, proud, frightened and vindictive creatures capable of unbelievably crude barbarism.

Any similarities which occur between the *Genesis* and the *Gilgamesh Epic* flood stories may be accounted for by the assumption that the latter has its roots in an oral tradition stretching right back to a literal, historic flood. Though subsequently evolving into pagan mythology, the surviving Babylonian legend of a great flood bears witness to a past reality. It is inconceivable that the writer of the overwhelmingly more sophisticated narrative of *Genesis* would have stolen anything from the primitive polytheistic legend. Far from such 'versions' undermining the *Genesis* record, we believe that the superior dignity, theology and language of the *Genesis* narrative marks it out as being inspired and true.

The Hittites

We pass through Room 54 and into Room 53 (the landing of the East Stairs). These two rooms form the Raymond and Beverly Sackler Gallery of Ancient Anatolia.

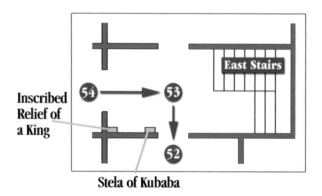

Stela of Kubaba

Left: Basalt stela of Hittite goddess Kubaba holding a mirror. Neo-Hittite, about 9th century BC from Carchemish [WA 125012], in Room 53.

Right: Inscribed basalt relief of a king. Neo-Hittite, about 730 BC, from Carchemish [WA 25003], in Room 53.

Here are remains of Hittite art, the Hittites being first mentioned in *Genesis 15*, and subsequently in numerous other passages (nearly 50 times). The best-known individual Hittite in the Bible is Uriah the husband of Bathsheba of *2 Samuel 11*. Joshua was given 'all the land of the Hittites' for conquest.

Because they were unknown to secular historians, the Hittites were dubbed 'a mythical people' and 'a figment of biblical imagination', but archaeological discovery (mainly in 1906 in Turkey) has provided considerable information about them. These mythical people of the Bible turned out to be a major force in the ancient world. Indeed, we now know that their empire once stretched from Mesopotamia to Syria and Palestine, and that they spoke in an Indo-European language. The examples of Hittite art on display here are from excavations at Carchemish.

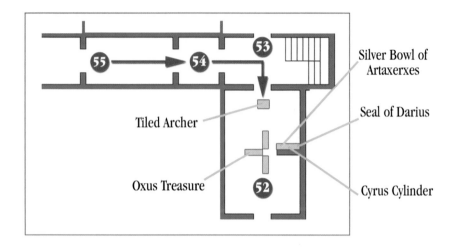

Esther, Nehemiah and the Persian Court 536–400 BC

Entering the Gallery of Ancient Iran (Room 52), we are confronted by a life-size *Tiled Archer* from the palace of Susa, called in the *King James Version,* 'Shushan the palace' (eg: *Nehemiah 1.1; Esther 1.2;* and *Daniel 8.2*). The palace at Susa was built in 490 BC by Darius the Great and was decorated with friezes of glazed painted tiles in moulded relief. This is one of the emperor's bodyguard of archers (known as Immortals), holding a spear. To Esther, the Jewess who in 479 BC became queen to Xerxes I, king of Persia (Ahasuerus in the Bible), this would have been a familiar figure.

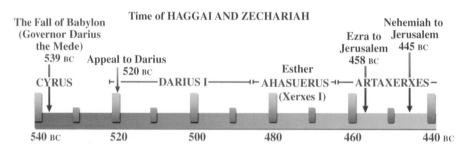

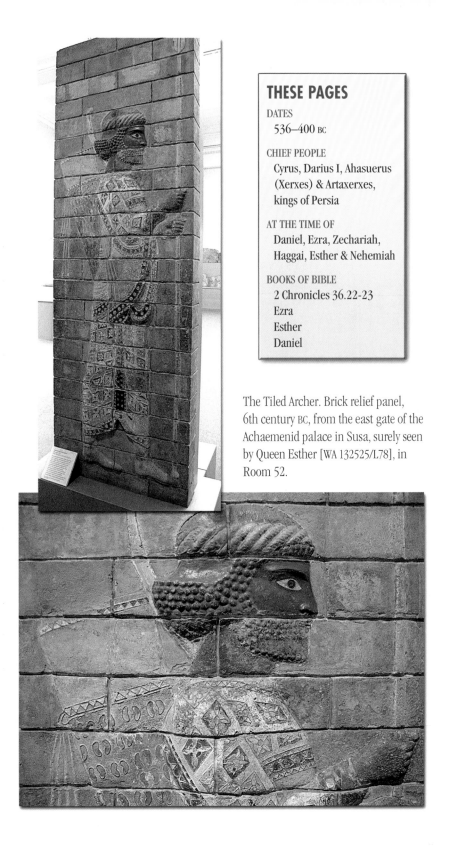

The Tiled Archer. Brick relief panel,
6th century BC, from the east gate of the
Achaemenid palace in Susa, surely seen
by Queen Esther [WA 132525/L78], in
Room 52.

The Cyrus Cylinder, about 9 inches long, inscribed by Cyrus the Great around 536 BC [Case 6 – WA 1880-6-17, 1941/90920], in Room 52

The Cyrus Cylinder

We proceed down the left-hand side of the Gallery of Ancient Iran looking for Case 6, exhibit 7.

This is the famous and priceless *Cyrus Cylinder,* barrel-shaped, clay, and inscribed in cuneiform. It speaks of the wickedness of Nabonidus, the last king of Babylon, and of how Cyrus took Babylon (in 539 BC) without bloodshed, merging the Babylonian empire with his own Medo-Persian dominions, confirming yet again the *Daniel* record. Cynical writers used to scoff at the idea that a sixth-century BC Persian emperor would be so politically sophisticated as to release captive peoples and declare religious liberty. The opening words of the book of *Ezra* were often derided:

BIBLE QUOTE

'Now in the first year of Cyrus king of Persia, that the word of the Lord by the mouth of Jeremiah might be fulfilled, the Lord stirred up the spirit of Cyrus king of Persia, that he made a proclamation throughout all his kingdom, and put it also in writing, saying, Thus saith Cyrus king of Persia, The Lord God of heaven hath given me all the kingdoms of the earth; and he hath charged me to build him an house at Jerusalem, which is in Judah. Who is there among you of all his people? his God be with him, and let him go up to Jerusalem . . . and build' *(Ezra 1.1-3).*

The discovery of the *Cyrus Cylinder* silenced criticism because it proclaims the policy of Cyrus (559-530 BC) to restore the liberty of foreign captives, and to encourage them to return home to worship according to their own traditions. It reads:

PERSIAN QUOTE

'As to the inhabitants of Babylon . . . I abolished the unpaid labour and denial of social standing . . . I brought relief to their derelict dwellings . . . I returned to the sacred cities on the other side of the Tigris (the sanctuaries of which had long been in ruins) the images which once lived in them and established for them *[the images]* permanent sanctuaries. I also gathered their former inhabitants and returned them . . . '

Excavations at Ur and Uruk (40 miles north-west of Ur) have also yielded up inscriptions stating that Cyrus personally authorised the restoration of temples in both these places. Thus the statements made in chapters 1 and 6 of *Ezra* (as well as in the closing verses of *2 Chronicles*) are authenticated from several local inscriptions as well as from the annals of Cyrus. While Cyrus released captives of all nationalities, re-establishing their national shrines, God overruled in his heart and moved him to realise the all-surpassing importance of doing this for the house of the God of Israel. The Bible once stood alone in telling this story, but now the records of contemporaries place the essential facts beyond challenge.

Seal of Darius the Great

Also in Case 6 is an official cylinder seal of Darius I – the *Agate Cylinder Seal* – bearing his title in old Persian, Elamite and Babylonian (the three official languages of the empire). It is possible that this is the Persian king's own seal, and if so, it would in all probability have appeared on the Temple project proclamation. The seal is positioned alongside its rolled out impression. It would have been used to emboss clay tablets to authenticate whatever had been inscribed in cuneiform script. This seal depicts Darius in his chariot confronting and shooting a threatening lion during a hunt.

First, it is helpful to know which Darius this is. After the fall of Babylon in 539 BC, a *regional* governor by the name of Darius ruled, serving under Cyrus. He is described in *Daniel 9* and also mentioned in chapters 6 and 11 where he is called 'Darius the Mede'. He is not the Darius of this seal. After the *regional* ruler of this name had passed from the scene another Darius came to prominence as king over the entire empire. This was Darius the Great, or Darius I, who ruled 521-486 BC. (Cyrus' own son committed suicide and Darius led a coup to take over.) During his reign the prophets Zechariah and Haggai ministered, and both mention him a number of times. So does Ezra (many times) as he records the rebuilding of

The Seal of Darius with trilingual cuneiform inscription in old Persian, Elamite and Babylonian [Case 6 – WA 1835-6-30,1/89132] in Room 52.

the Temple *(Ezra 5-6)*. When obstructionists brought to a halt the rebuilding of the Temple an appeal was made to Darius I (in 520 BC). He ordered a full investigation of the archives and found the original decree of Cyrus authorising the project. Darius made a new proclamation together with a total rebuilding grant *(Ezra 6.8)*.

Darius I maintained the policy inaugurated by Cyrus of encouraging foreign nationals to return to their homelands and to pursue their own religions. In an adjacent case we can view silver tableware of the kind used at Esther's table.

Remains at Persepolis, secondary palace to Susa, built by Darius I where the king could sit in an audience hall 200 feet long and 65 feet high.

The Silver Bowl of Artaxerxes I, 5th century BC [ANE 1994-1-27,1] in Room 52

Silver Bowl of Artaxerxes

In Case 7 there is a *Silver Bowl of Artaxerxes* inscribed: 'Son of Xerxes, son of Darius'. Xerxes is the Persian king known in the Bible as Ahasuerus, the son of Darius the Great. All three kings are referred to in *Ezra 4*.

Xerxes (Ahasuerus) succeeded his father Darius in 486 BC, ruling an immense empire from India to Ethiopia. In the record of the Bible, he deposed his queen, Vashti, replacing her in time with Esther. In 465 BC, after a 21-year reign, and some 14 years after taking Esther as his queen, he was assassinated, his son Artaxerxes (465-424 BC) succeeding him. It was Artaxerxes who brought the rebuilding of Jerusalem to a temporary halt *(Ezra 4.7-23)*, and who

Grandeur of the ruins of Persepolis, created by Darius I

commissioned Ezra to visit the city as a kind of secretary of state for Jewish affairs in 458 BC. Thirteen years later this same king dispatched Nehemiah, his cup-bearer (a member of the inner cabinet), to Jerusalem as civil governor. Artaxerxes was generally very kindly disposed to the Jews. To summarise: one silver bowl commemorates three Persian kings prominent in biblical history.

The Oxus Treasure

The *Oxus Treasure* is displayed in three central cases in this room, consisting of magnificent items from the fifth to third centuries BC showing the immense wealth of the Persian court. All this confirms the portrayal of court splendour in the book of *Esther*. Such objects were part of the environment of the queen, and also, later, of Nehemiah. The treasure takes its name from the River Oxus, having been found at the site of an ancient city on its banks. Visitors may wish to view these objects, although time is limited as much remains to be seen.

Daily Life in Ancient Egypt

From Room 52 we retrace our steps back to Room 53 and straight across the landing to Room 65 – the Egypt and Africa Gallery.

Egypt and Africa
Ancient Iran
East Stairs
65
52
53
64
Egyptian Funerary Archaeology
63
62
59
61
Understanding Ancient Egyptian Culture
West Stairs
73-71
The Wolfson Gallery Rome: City and Empire
70
Life in Ancient Greece and Rome
69
The Money Gallery
68

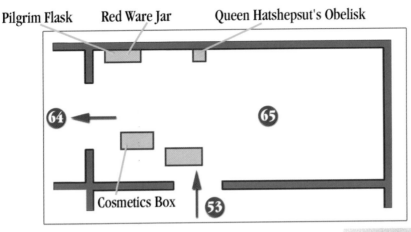

Pilgrim Flask   Red Ware Jar   Queen Hatshepsut's Obelisk

64 ← 65

Cosmetics Box 53

Here are exhibits roughly corresponding with the years that the children of Israel were in Egypt from **1876 BC (in Joseph's lifetime) to 1446 BC**, the time of the Exodus. Nothing here proves the presence of the Israelites in Egypt, but the biblical narrative is shown to be wholly authentic in its descriptions.

Directly ahead across the room is *Queen Hatshepsut's Obelisk*. Hatshepsut (around the 1550s to 1483 BC) was the daughter of Pharaoh Tuthmosis I, who probably issued the two decrees that all Israelite baby boys be killed. If so, it was Hatshepsut who rescued Moses. A noted historian wrote: 'only she of all known women of the period possessed the presumption and independence to violate an ordinance of the king, and under his very nose at that.' She married her younger half-brother who became Tuthmosis II. Moses, by this construction, was her 'foster-son'.

Red granite obelisk inscribed with the name of Queen Hatshepsut. Rescuer and foster-mother of Moses, she was 'one of the most fascinating and influential persons of all Egyptian history'. 'By faith Moses, when he was come to years, refused to be called the son of Pharaoh's daughter' *(Hebrews 11.24)*. [EA 1834] Room 65.

Top left: Red ware jar, about 1500-1480 BC
[Case 8 – EA 72320] in Room 65

Top right: Cosmetics box of ebony, inlaid
with ivory and faience plaques, about
1550-1295 BC [Case 1 – EA 5897] in Room 65

Right: Cream coated marl ware pilgrim
flask, about 1350-1250 BC [Case 8 – EA
65685] in Room 65

In a case to the left of *Queen Hatshepsut's Obelisk* is an interesting cream coated marl ware pilgrim flask dated between 1350-1250 BC (100 years after the Exodus), and a red ware jar, dated between 1500-1480 BC.

In an island display case to the left of the door (leading out to Room 64) is a beautiful cosmetics box of ebony, which could be as old as the birth of 'Queen Hattie', the very kind of luxury familiar to Moses in his early life in the Egyptian royal palace.

We move into Room 64 (Early Egypt) and walk straight through into Room 63 (unless a glance at the display on pyramids is of interest).

Room 65 – Egypt and Africa

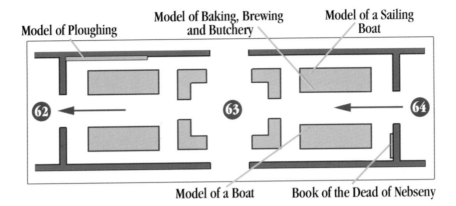

Model of Ploughing **Model of Baking, Brewing and Butchery** **Model of a Sailing Boat**

Model of a Boat **Book of the Dead of Nebseny**

Room 63 (Funerary Archaeology) contains many items illustrating Egyptian life at the time the children of Israel were there, showing the authenticity of the descriptions in *Genesis* and *Exodus*.

To the left of the door as you enter is the *Book of the Dead of Nebseny*. An island display case nearby contains a painted wooden model boat, and the opposite case has a model of a sailing boat. The same case has a model representing baking, brewing and butchery, while in the far right-hand corner of the room is a model showing a peasant ploughing. All the models were found in tombs.

Book of the Dead of Nebseny, showing spells buried with a dead person to help him through the perils of the afterlife to the place of happiness. Even Egyptian heathenism grasped by instinct that the 'happy place' must be deserved; [Case 2 – EA 9900/6] in Room 63.

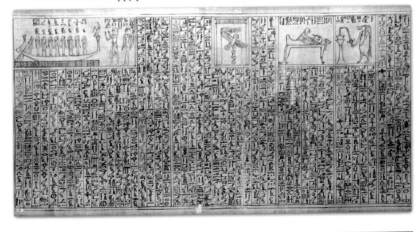

Room 63 – Funerary Archaeology

Painted Wooden Funerary Models

Clockwise from top left: Model representing baking, brewing and butchery, 2000-1970 BC [Case 5 – EA 41576]; model of a sailing boat, 1985-1795 BC [Case 5 – EA 41574]; model boat [Case 4 – EA 35293]; model of peasant ploughing, c. 2025 BC [Case 11 – EA 51091]. All in Room 63.

Leaving Room 63 at the opposite end to our entry, we pass into and through Room 62, to enter Room 61 – Understanding Ancient Egyptian Culture.

We note Case 35 immediately before us, and look for the mud brick stamped with the cartouche of Ramesses II (with straw showing). This pharaoh lived nearly 150 years after the Exodus, but the brick would have been the same as those made by the forced labour of the Israelites in Egypt.

Case 18 on the long side wall contains a manual for interpreting dreams. (We remember the importance of dreams in the history of Joseph.) Various cases show jewellery, writing and domestic materials. Case 38 has a model of brickmakers (the work of the captive children of Israel).

All these exhibits provide an impression of the culture of Egypt from Joseph to Moses, confirming as historically correct the descriptions of *Genesis* and *Exodus*.

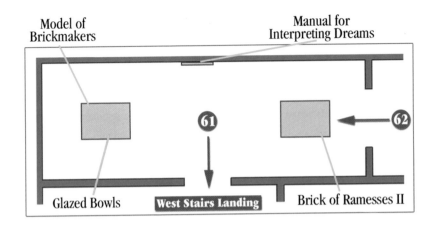

Model of Brickmakers

Manual for Interpreting Dreams

61

62

Glazed Bowls

West Stairs Landing

Brick of Ramesses II

Above: Manual for interpreting dreams, so important to the ancient Egyptians [Case 18 – EA 10683.3] in Room 61

Right: Wooden funerary model of brickmakers c.1900 BC [Case 38 – EA 63837] in Room 61

Below: Mud brick stamped with the cartouche of Ramesses II, 1279-1213 BC [Case 35 – EA 6020] in Room 61

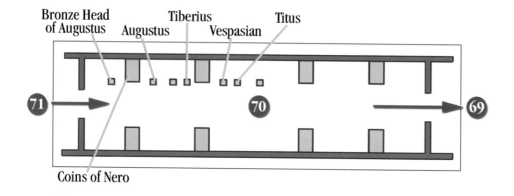

Bronze Head of Augustus · Augustus · Tiberius · Vespasian · Titus

71   70   69

Coins of Nero

Daily Life in New Testament Times

From Room 61, we cross the landing of the West Stairs, and move swiftly through Greek and Roman galleries to Room 70 – The Wolfson Gallery, Rome: City and Empire.

Here we see the sculptures of Roman emperors who ruled during the life of Christ and the early New Testament period. These are undoubtedly good likenesses. Two coins from Nero's reign may also be seen in this room. It was during his reign that the apostles Peter and Paul were executed.

Coins of Nero, Roman Emperor (AD 54-68)
Left: Nero's food market, minted AD 64-68 [Case 3 – CM 1864.11.28.251], in Room 70
Right: The Triumphal Arch of Nero, minted AD 64-68 [Case 3 – CM 1872.7-9.454], in Room 70

Room 70 – Rome: City and Empire

Left: **Augustus** (reigned 27 BC–AD 14). Caesar at the time of the birth of Christ, initiated the census just before His birth. During his reign a golden age of Roman architecture and literature flourished. Founded the famous Praetorian Guard [GR 1879.7-12.9]; in Room 70.

Right: **Tiberius** (reigned AD 14-37). Caesar during the earthly ministry of Christ. In AD 26 he appointed Pontius Pilate governor of Judea. Jewish disturbances would have caused Tiberius to remove Pilate from office, and Pilate was mindful of this when Jewish leaders threatened to inform Caesar if Christ was released [GR 1812.6-15.2]; in Room 70.

Left: **Vespasian** (reigned AD 69-79). Effectively successor to Nero, this frugal, efficient ruler rebuilt the economy and also cities crippled by earthquakes (such as some in *Revelation 2-3*) [GR 1850.3-4.35]; in Room 70.

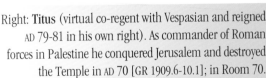

Right: **Titus** (virtual co-regent with Vespasian and reigned AD 79-81 in his own right). As commander of Roman forces in Palestine he conquered Jerusalem and destroyed the Temple in AD 70 [GR 1909.6-10.1]; in Room 70.

We proceed into Room 69 – the Life in Ancient Greece and Rome Gallery. Here are many fascinating objects, most of which would have been familiar to people in the time of Christ and the first century, including 'Doctor Luke's instruments'.

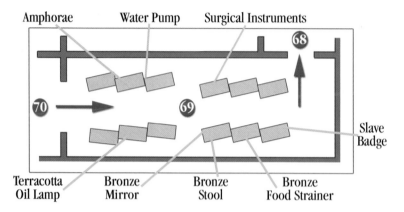

Typical transport amphorae (two-handled vessels) [Case 14 – GR1756.1-226/1132 ; 1805.7-3.219; 1904.2-4.1451; 1848.6-19.9] in Room 69

Top left: Bronze mirror [Case 9 – GR 1898.7-16.4] in Room 69

Top right: Bronze food strainer [Case 11 – GR 1814.7-4.712] in Room 69

Middle right: Terracotta oil lamp [Case 19 – GR 1856.12-26.479] in Room 69

Bottom left: Bronze stool [Case 10 – GR 1856.12-26.667] in Room 69

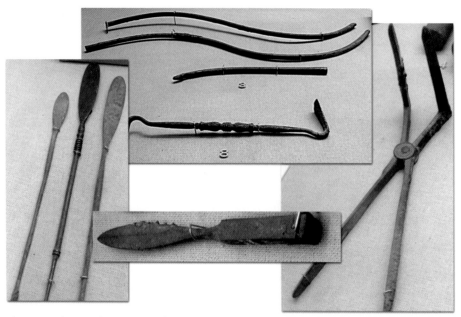

Above: Set of surgical instruments from the time of Luke, including (clockwise from left) spatulae used for mixing and applying ointments; catheters and a double-ended blunt hook; a rectal speculum; and a scalpel handle, 1st century AD [Case 3 – GR 1968.6-26. 1 to 39] in Room 69.

Below: Bronze double-action water pump, probably 3rd century AD, later than the NT period, but showing the sophistication of the wealthy [Case 13 – GR 1892.5-17.1], in Room 69.

Roman slave badge. The words say: 'Seize me if I should try to escape and return me to my Master, Viventius on the estate of Callistus' (probably in Rome). Also used for dogs!

Onesimus, the runaway slave of Philemon of Colossae, would probably have worn such a badge [Case 7 – GR 1975.9.26], in Room 69.

We go next into Room 68 – the Money Gallery, where interesting coins from various rulers of biblical times are displayed. For want of time we look only at a few, the first being in Case 3 and panel 3, where a *denarius* is shown from the reign of Tiberius Caesar. This is probably the very kind of denarius featured in *Matthew 22.19-21*. 'Shew me the tribute money,' said Christ.

BIBLE QUOTE

'And they brought unto him a penny. And he saith unto them, Whose is this image and superscription? They say unto him, Caesar's. Then saith he unto them, Render therefore unto Caesar the things which are Caesar's; and unto God the things that are God's.'

Denarius of Tiberius (AD 14-37) known as the 'Tribute Penny' [Case 3, Nos 20 & 21], in Room 68

Our second coin to view is on panel 4, numbers 36 and 37, this being a coin of Titus commemorating the destruction of Jerusalem in AD 70 (the 'formal end' of the Jewish church). A gold coin of Augustus and a bronze coin of Nero may also be viewed in this case.

Above: Bronze coin of the Emperor Titus commemorating the 'capture of Jerusalem' [Case 3, Nos 36 & 37] in Room 68
Below left: Bronze coin of Nero (AD 54-68) [Case 3, No 14] in Room 68
Below right: Gold coin of Augustus (27 BC-AD 14) [Case 3, No 28] in Room 68

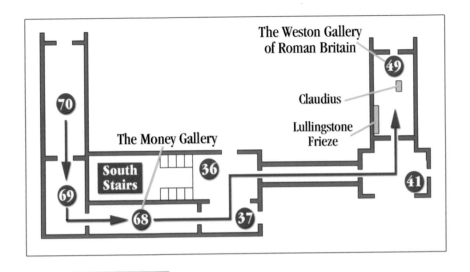

Roman Britain

From Room 68 we proceed into Room 37 and turn left onto the landing of the South Stairs. Before going downstairs visitors may like to digress for a moment to view the Lullingstone wall decorations. These are decorations from the earliest known Christian chapel in this country in the fourth century AD. From the landing of the South Stairs (Room 36) follow the corridor into Room 41. From here, turn left into Room 49, the Weston Gallery of Roman Britain.

At Lullingstone in Kent a Roman villa had its top floor converted into a chapel provided with its own outside public staircase and entrance. In the nineteenth century, part of the mosaic floor of this Roman villa was discovered when a fence was erected, and in 1949 a full excavation was begun by Lieutenant Colonel G. W. Meates. The villa (following a fifth-century fire) had been abandoned, the upper floors collapsing into the basement. With many pots and wall decorations now reassembled, and the history of the villa traced, it is evident that a wealthy Roman family practised pagan rites in an adjoining temple and in basement rooms. However, from the fourth century the occupying Roman family embraced Christianity, and the upper floor 'house church' was prepared – decorations showing

Above: Colonel Meates' reconstruction of Lullingstone Roman Villa.

Opposite page top right: Six similar figures whose outstretched arms indicate an attitude of prayer. Restored from numerous fragments of painted wall-plaster, they originally formed a continuous frieze along one wall of a room in the Lullingstone Roman Villa, 4th century AD; [PRB 1967.4-7.1] in Room 49.

Left: Detail from the Lullingstone frieze. Height of figure approximately 28 inches.

a family at prayer, with the chi-rho monogram with alpha and omega letters, the distinctive Christian symbols. We show here Colonel Meates' reconstruction of the villa (not in the Museum). Christianity was clearly established in Britain by this time through the Roman occupation and business travelling. A famous and

beautiful Christian mosaic courtyard is nearby, from Dorset, which was originally laid in the fourth century AD. Other artefacts are to be seen, but time is now very limited and there are more exhibits to view on the lower floor.

The Emperor Claudius (AD 41-54) who followed mad Caligula and preceded Nero. Claudius ended persecution of Jews and extended Herod Agrippa's kingdom, but later expelled all Jews from Rome (Aquila and Priscilla among them); [Case 14 – PRB 1965.12-1.1] in Room 49.

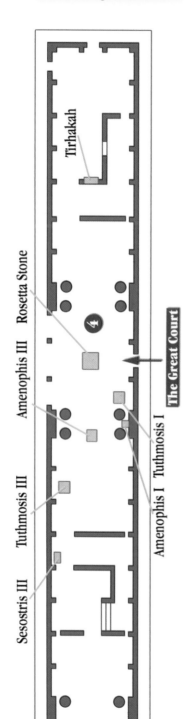

Sesostris III
Reigned 1878–1843 BC
He may have been the ruler who welcomed Jacob
and his sons to settle in Egypt in the eastern
Delta. Joseph was his prime minister.

'And Pharaoh said unto Joseph, Say unto thy brethren,
This do ye; lade your beasts, and go, get you unto the land of
Canaan; and take your father and your households, and come
unto me: and I will give you the good of the land of Egypt,
and ye shall eat the fat of the land' *(Genesis 45.17-18)*.

The Pharaohs and Bible Events

From Room 49, we retrace our steps to the landing of the South Stairs (the enormous staircase leading down to the main entrance area) and descend to the ground floor. (Lifts are adjacent.)

Here we have a choice, either to turn left to visit the Great Court and see the historic Reading Room (not to mention the Court Restaurant or Café), or to travel through the Great Court left side to access for the second time Room 4 (Egyptian Sculpture) for a glance at several significant pharaohs and the *Rosetta Stone.*

The information that we give here about the dates of the pharaohs is based on the conclusions of the *Cambridge Ancient History* (third edition), a very reputable scheme of dates. Such dates cannot be established with certainty, and between various authorities figures vary by up to thirty years for the pharaohs we shall view. It will be noticed that our dates differ from those shown by the Museum, but the *Cambridge* dates agree well with great biblical events. Nothing here provides direct corroboration of any named biblical person or event, but it is interesting to see sculptures of the powerful rulers who may well have been those interacting with the children of Israel in the biblical record.

Rosetta Stone

Pride of place in the centre of the gallery is given to the famous *Rosetta Stone.* Nearly four feet high, this black basalt stone was found at Rosetta in Egypt in 1799 by Napoleon's soldiers. It carries a citation in three versions of writing – Egyptian hieroglyphics (top), demotic or popular Egyptian (centre), and Greek (bottom), providing the means for the first deciphering of ancient Egyptian hieroglyphics. All Museum visitors want to see this milestone discovery in the development of archaeology.

Room 4 – Egyptian Sculpture

EA 683
in Room 4

Amenophis I (also called Amenhotep I)
Reigned 1546–1526 BC
If we accept the traditional early date of the Exodus, calculated by the Bible's own figures, then the Exodus occurred in 1446 BC, and the birth of Moses eighty years before in 1526 BC. If our chosen dates for Amenophis I are correct, then he would be the king referred to in *Exodus 1.8-14* – the pharaoh of the oppression. It could also have been he who ordered the death of the Hebrew baby boys, although this decree, and the birth of Moses, could well have taken place at the beginning of the reign of the next king – Tuthmosis I.

EA 1238
in Room 4

Tuthmosis I
Reigned 1526–1512 BC
This pharaoh may have ordered the death of the baby boys *(Exodus 1.15-22)*. His daughter Hatshepsut would then have been the one who rescued Moses *(Exodus 2.5-10)* and became his foster-mother. She would have been in her teens. She later married her younger half-brother, Tuthmosis II, who died mysteriously in his late twenties.

EA 61 in Room 4

Tuthmosis III (Some think this is Amenophis II, see next page)

Reigned 1504–1450 BC

The first twenty years of his reign were dominated by his mother-in-law Queen Hatshep-sut. But she was probably near to death and void of influence when Moses went into exile in 1486 BC, aged forty, to avoid the murderous intentions of this pharaoh *(Exodus 2.15)*. Tuthmosis III may well have been warily jealous of Moses, who was older than he.

EA 3 in Room 4

Amenophis III

Reigned 1417–1379 BC

Ruled during Israel's occupation of Canaan under Joshua, but neither Amenophis III nor his son were interested in defending their territories there. Some of the Amarna Letters written to these pharaohs by the kings and officials of Canaanite city-states plead for deliverance from the enemy (most probably the Israelites) taking over the land.

Amenophis II

Reigned 1450–1425 BC

This pharaoh cannot be viewed at present. He was, according to our chosen dates, the pharaoh of the Exodus, which took place in 1446 BC – not Ramesses II as often asserted. (The latter reigned much later.)

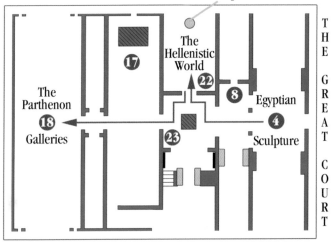

Column from the Temple of Artemis

The Hellenistic World

The Parthenon

Galleries

Egyptian

Sculpture

THE GREAT COURT

Temple of Diana at Ephesus and the Elgin Marbles

From Room 4, housing the pharaohs, visitors may wish to view these nearby exhibits. They do not validate any biblical events but provide an interesting background impression, if time is no problem. Follow the map to Room 23, and through to Room 22 where there is a massive base of a column from the Temple of Artemis (Diana) in Ephesus, the goddess mentioned in *Acts 19*. Paul's preaching led to a violent mob reaction, stirred up by the makers of shrines for Diana.

Proceed to Room 18 to view the *Elgin Marbles* from the Parthenon in Athens, built in the 5th century BC, and dominating the city. Paul's whole being was repelled by all that the Parthenon represented, as well as by the many other pagan shrines in Athens. The architecture is unquestionably glorious, and the sculptures a work of human genius, but *Acts 17* tells us that Paul's spirit was stirred in him, when he saw the city wholly given over to idolatry. In the course of his remonstrating with groups of people he was invited by the philosophers of Athens to preach the sermon reported in *Acts 17.22-32* on Mars' Hill. We doubt that Paul ever set foot in the

Parthenon, any more than Christians would care to enter an active pagan temple today, and we also doubt whether he would have taken time to view the high level sculptures with their pagan and immodest character. However, if time permits, a passing look at these sculptures will provide a vivid impression of the superstition that ruled the lives of Athenians.

The Politarch Inscription 2nd century AD

This exhibit is included at the end of this guide because it is unusual for Room 78 on the lower floor, where it is exhibited, to be open. It is also quite a trek to get to it. It is a significant vindication of Luke's record in *Acts*. Intrepid visitors may wish to try.

In *Acts 17.6* and *8*, Luke calls the city officials at Thessalonica 'politarchs' (translated 'rulers of the city' in the *KJV*). This term was absent from Greek literature, and so prior to 1835 critics of the Bible did not hesitate to call Luke an unreliable historian. However, in 1835 the title 'POLITARCH' with a list of rulers' names was found on a 2nd century AD inscription on an arch in Thessalonica (pictured below, GR 1877.5-11.1), proving that Luke was right and reliable after all. The Bible is always vindicated in the end. Similar inscriptions have turned up in other places subsequently.

There are many more confirmations of the accuracy of the Bible in other museums. The following pages present just a few.

The Temple Warning Notice AD 31
In the Archaeological Museum, Istanbul

In *Acts 21.28-29* we read of how the Jews seized Paul in the Temple at Jerusalem and stirred up the people to fury, charging him with having brought Gentiles into the Temple – 'For they had seen before with him in the city Trophimus an Ephesian, whom they supposed that Paul had brought into the temple.' They were about to kill him when he was rescued by the Roman military, leading to imprisonment, many examinations, and trial in Rome. The *Temple Warning Notice* was found in 1871 at the site of the Temple, and is dated AD 31. Positioned on a four-foot high marble wall separating the outer court of the Temple area from the rest, it is written in Greek only, as it does not apply to Jews. It warns –

TEMPLE QUOTE

'No Gentile may enter the enclosing screen around the Temple. Whoever is caught will have himself to blame that his death results.'

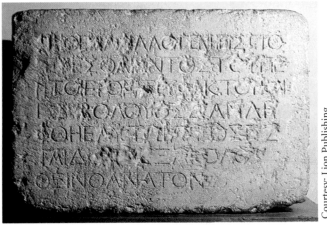

Courtesy: Lion Publishing

Evidence from other museums

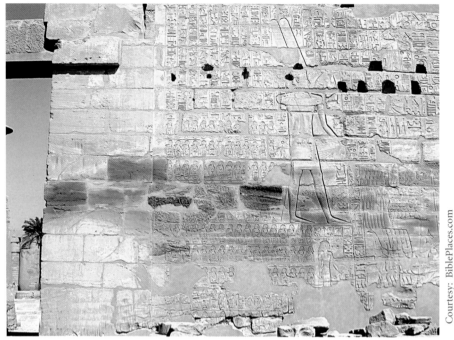

'Shishak's' city list on his temple wall in Karnak

Pharaoh's Calling Card Confirms an Invasion 926 BC

The *Stela of Shoshenk I* and his Karnak city list confirm an event that took place in 926 BC, shortly after the time of Solomon. The Bible relates how Rehoboam, king of Judah, suffered an invasion by Pharaoh Shoshenk I of Egypt, called Shishak in the *King James Version*. Shoshenk took fortified cities, coming to the very wall of Jerusalem, plundering the Temple, taking off the rich treasuries of gold. All this is in *1 Kings 14.25-8* and *2 Chronicles 12.2-12*. Shoshenk left a list of towns attacked inscribed in stone on the south wall of his temple in Karnak (ancient Thebes), near Luxur. Included among many towns of Israel was Megiddo, where later excavations found a broken commemorative stone bearing Shoshenk's name. The conqueror had left his calling card in the ruins. So a pharaoh provided double evidence for a piece of Bible history.

Letters from the Nile Confirm
Ezra 500–400 BC In the Brooklyn Museum

The *Elephantine Papyri* consist of numerous letters and contracts found on the island of Elephantine in the Nile, near Aswan, Egypt. The island was a Jewish garrison community called the 'Yeb Fortress', peopled by descendants of soldiers and civilian workers. The letters and contracts, wonderfully preserved in the dry climate of Egypt, include loan agreements and property transfer deeds. They were written between 500-400 BC in a style of Aramaic identical to that used for writing to the Persian king (plus five other 'official' letters or documents) in the book of *Ezra,* clearly the lingua franca of the empire at that time. The authenticity of *Ezra* (long impugned) was emphatically confirmed when these documents began to appear in the 1890s. One very significant letter written to the priests in Jerusalem speaks of Delaiah and Shelemiah, the sons of Sanballat, then still alive, who figures prominently in the book of *Nehemiah.* The high priest Johanan, also in *Nehemiah,* is referred to. Such references tie the books of *Ezra* and *Nehemiah* to the world of the Elephantine garrison community, both in culture and period.

Aramaic documents from Elephantine, 404 BC. The top is a marriage contract, the bottom conveys a house from father to daughter. Courtesy: Brooklyn Museum, USA.

Early Fragment of John's Gospel AD 125-150
In the John Ryland's Library, Manchester

It is often thought that the Bible must have changed greatly through many years of copying from manuscript to manuscript. If it were a purely human work, this would no doubt be the case. We have already noted that the *Dead Sea Scrolls*, which include 2nd century BC scriptures, have shown the astonishingly accurate preservation of the Old Testament, and here we see an example of a New Testament fragment. Such fragments confirm the accuracy of the transmission of the New Testament text, and this is the earliest of them. Written in Greek and dated by experts at AD 125-150, it bears on one side John's Gospel chapter 18, verses 31-33, and on the other verses 37-38. It is clearly a page of a book (a codex), and not part of a scroll. Christians were evidently using the book format long before it became general for Greek literature.

This fragment contains Pilate's famous question, 'What is truth?', and also the words of Christ: 'Every one that is of the truth heareth my voice.' What better words are there to bring to a close a review of evidence for the inspired and infallible Bible. Its history is always verified by archaeological discovery, and its message of new life from Christ is always proved true by the experience of those who trust in Him.

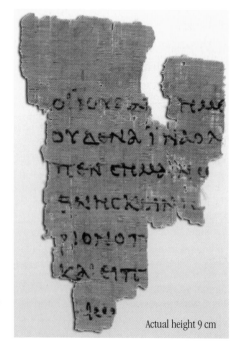

Actual height 9 cm

Index of Names and Places

Index of Artefacts

* Denotes items which are not in the
British Museum